Tausha

The Life and Teachings of a Russian Mystic

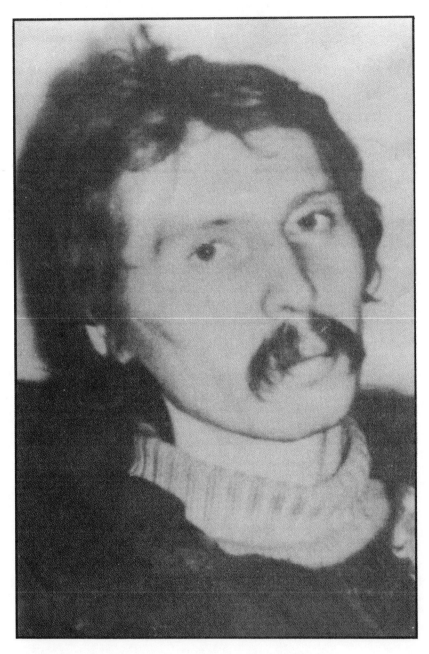

KGB photograph of Tausha taken when he was arrested in 1985

Tausha

The Life and Teachings of a Russian Mystic

ILIA BELIAEV

STATION HILL

BARRYTOWN, LTD.

Published by Station Hill / Barrytown, Ltd.
in Barrytown, New York 12507.

E-mail: publishers@stationhill.org
Online catalogue: http://www.stationhill.org

Station Hill Arts is a project of The Institute for Publishing Arts, Inc., a not-for-profit, federally tax exempt organization in Barrytown, New York, which gratefully acknowledges ongoing support for its publishing program from the New York State Council on the Arts.

Typesetting and design by Susan Quasha
Front cover photograph by Susan Quasha

Library of Congress Cataloging-in-Publication Data

Beliaev, Ilia, 1954-
  Tausha : the life and teachings of a Russian mystic / Ilia Beliaev .
    p. cm.
  ISBN 1-58177-024-3 (alk. Paper)
  1. Tausha. 2. Mystics—Soviet Union—Biography. 3. Spiritual Biography—Soviet Union. I. Title.
  BL73.T37 B45 2000
  291.4'092—dc21
                                99-087510

Manufactured in the United States of America

To Victoria

Acknowledgments

Many thanks for this book are due to Pierre Chicoine and Madame Z, Robert Dubiel, June Rouse, Andrea Kuo, Julie Simmons, George Quasha, and Charles Stein, whose participation made this book possible.

Foreword

Stephen Larsen

Tausha has a unique quality that is like a haunting memory from a soul-stirring time or place, a mingling of scents on the air, an image pregnant with meaning, a warm sensation around the heart. It narrates a journey exquisitely painful in places, but never uninteresting. For the spiritual literati, the settings are exotic enough: from the warrens of St. Petersburg to a mysterious camp by the Black Sea, to hermit-inhabited mountain grottoes in Georgia. One feels the shade of Gurdjieff moving in parallel orbits nearby. There he was, a few decades earlier, setting an archetypal dance in motion: the legend-creating actions of that mysterious being we might call the trickster/shaman/guru. The author stands in the proper, time-honored relation to this figure: Ouspensky to Gurdjieff, Kyriakos Markides to Daskalos, Castaneda to Don Juan, Ilia to Tausha.

But there is a blight on the land: the soul-stultifying grey of the secular collective mind and the police state. Orwell evoked it aptly enough in his fantasy, *1984*, but here we have real modern lives being lived against this bleak, existentially terrifying backdrop. Moreover, we can immediately identify with Ilia Beliaev's characters and with the character who is the author himself; for this book is a genuine autobiographical account of the wonders and terrors of a spiritual quest taking place under a curse that has befallen the entire country like a curse in a fairytale. Under its spell, the human soul longs for a universe that makes sense, longs for that sweet connectedness, that homecoming that is the goal of every spiritual quest.

I and my colleagues in the social sciences wondered what must really be going on behind the scenes in Russia during the 1960s, when *Psychic Discoveries Behind the Iron Curtain* was published. That book presented a mind-boggling paradox: Here we were, members of a "free" society, going to the land of thought control and Big Brother, to find out what the unfettered human mind is really capable of! How could this be? Behind the "ironest" of curtains there lurked, it seemed, clairvoyants, telepaths, people who could move objects with their minds and foretell the future. In the mythological corner of my own mind, I imagined a scene from the national epic of Finland, *The Kalevala*: we see a room in an innocent-looking farmhouse that to ordinary eyes is full of ordinary people; a fire is blazing, a kettle is on the hearth. But to the second sight of the epic's poet, the place is full of shamans: invisible magical duels are being fought all over the room; the portals to the astral are open and spirit-presences are peering benevolently or balefully into this world. "Wizards in the woodwork, and sitting on the rafters," *The Kalevala* says. Though gathered from Finnish legends, I think that *The Kalevala* is speaking as well about an indomitable, indigenous, pan-Russian mysticism.

It is almost an anthropological cliché that the Northern climate is conducive to a visionary temperament. Anthropologists, trying to explain the circumpolar distribution of shamanic societies, demean them with the term "arctic hysteria"! The mind, confronted by the arctic vastness and the long winter nights, breeds chimaeras; people become shamans—or simply go mad. Russia herself, but also the Ukraine, the Balkan states, Georgia, all have their indigenous lineages of mystics and healers—lineages that are not broken just because they are socially forbidden—in fact they gain strength through confrontation with their nemeses. The beautiful poignancy of *Tausha* lies in the seriousness and inner compulsion of its protagonist's spiritual quest conducted against a social backdrop that is totally inimical to it—one in which psychics are only useful if they are useful to the state! (But perhaps this outright socialist agenda is actually less destructive than the alternative—the materialistic "scientism" that predominates in the "free" world and that denies the very existence of spiritual realities, not because they are socially pernicious, but because they are impregnable to the scientifically socialized mind. For the dominant paradigm, they simply don't exist!)

In 1992, my wife Robin and I attended a conference of the International Transpersonal Association in Prague, Czechoslovakia. The ITA supports the principles of Transpersonal Psychology: basically the view that the spiritual perspective has an important contribution to make to our understanding of the psyche and the human situation in general. Many of the presenters, like founder Stanislav Grof, had begun under the materialistic (Freudian/Darwinian) paradigm, and found themselves unable to explain certain findings without opening their theoretical model to include the universality of mind and Spirit and the interconnectedness of all things.

It was late spring in Prague. The years of Soviet oppression were finally over, and the innately romantic, artistic, and boisterous Czech spirit was just beginning to reassert herself. The ancient squares and parks were in blossom. It was as if Sleeping Beauty were finally awakening. I was having a good time smiling at people in the subways—to see if they still had the muscles! The results were sometimes dubious, sometimes absolutely delightful. One warm afternoon we were at a meeting at venerable Charles University, when we realized the room was unbearably stuffy. I asked for the windows to be opened. There was an awkward pause, and we were reminded that a terror of eavesdropping still lingered from the days of Soviet oppression—the fear of being overheard saying politically incorrect things. Suddenly Ivan Havel, a noted Czech physicist (and Vaclav's brother) and I looked at each other and said, "Let's open the windows!" We leaped up into the ancient three-foot thick window wells and pried the creaking windows open. It was both a physical and a symbolic event. Everybody cheered and applauded, and nobody even got "defenestrated" (the ancient Czech custom of throwing a *persona non grata* out the window).

Another moment of poignancy came when a Russian mathematician told his story. His mathematics supported a theory which implied that everything in the universe is interconnected. This was thought by the Soviets to be inconsistent with dialectical materialism and the social platform, so he was asked to redo the mathematics to make it yield an acceptable result—or he would go to the Gulag. The mathematics proved intractable, however, so off he went. They periodically released him on probation to see if his mathematics had learned its lesson, but it never did. He felt he had hit on a fundamentally incontrovertible theorem, which had as an implication (not unlike Einstein's relativity theory) the interconnectedness of all things. He spent 20 years in the work camps and suffered immensely in the service of truth. Now, in front of three-hundred transpersonal psychologists, for the first time able to present the truth as he saw it, he wept for joy, and the audience wept with him. He received a standing ovation, and dozens of people seemed intent on undoing the bleakness and loneliness of all those years in the Gulag with hugs and the time-honored balm of laughter and tears.

Europe has always pictured Russia as a place of mystics and wild fanatics; it is the portal to the wilds—the arctic, the forest, the Steppes—but it is also a gateway to the Orient. I was aware as I read *Tausha*, how present the Orient is in this book—the shaman-lands that lie to the remote East, the lands of the Buryat, of the Goldi with their magnificent costumes, and of the Tungus, from whose language the term "shaman" comes. The word is cognate with the Sanskrit "shramana" or long-eared yogi—India is present in this book too, as Ilia discovered his thirst for the spiritual while reading the biographies of Sri Ramakrishna, Sri Aurobindo, and Yogananda; so is Tibet, the land of the lamas on the northwestern escarpment of the Himalayas, now under its own foreign oppression; and so is that no-where-land of the ever-renewed spiritual promise, which is itself very palpable in these pages: Shambhala.

If we are sensitive, as Beliaev is, to the mythology alive in the Russian landscape, we see, through the bleak Soviet sociopolitical gloss, the true lineaments of the land of Russia: a country with a great heart, with grandeur in its vastness and a wilderness too large for human oppression. Ancient ruins still beckon as places to enact rituals; they are apertures for the sacred to break forth and bless everyday life. And there are mountains where hermits are still venerated, and where the traditions of saints and holy monks are still alive. We are initiated in this book to a sacred landscape that will always outlast the secular, for it breathes miracles and legends, and they are what stay in the soul.

We are also initiated into spiritual practices in *Tausha*; it provides specific instructions in magical and meditative techniques, as well as narrating spiritually instructive events. But Tausha himself does not proselytize for any particular tradition. For instance, Christ and the Buddha are equally venerated; though there is a different practice related to each figure: Ilia is instructed to venerate the Buddha, but not pray to him. The Buddha came and went leaving (iconographically for the first three centuries) only footprints, empty thrones and parasols, from China to the Gobi. Buddha is the one who came and went, instructing us in emptiness. Christ offered himself as an intermediary between humankind and the unfathomable godhead. Therefore you should direct your prayers to him.

This book is full of hope, despite the pain and human tragedy it chronicles so faithfully. One feels Ilia's integrity, the intensity of his quest, and its underlying reason. His incredulity is ours, his questioning, disappointment, bitterness, ours. The spiritual quest without these things is a Disney fantasy, a two-dimensional charade without guts and heart. This book has both, and it may empower us to find our own relation to the vicissitudes of the spiritual journey. It is hard to finish this book without coming to know Tausha enough to empathize, love, and grieve for him. Knowing that, read on!

Preface

There is a Great Wish living in our heart. It is the wish to go back to our eternal Home. How can we find it? Where is the path? Where but among our wishes themselves?

Our wishes are the basis for our actions. By those actions we create our karma, reap what we have sown, and find ourselves in the place and circumstances where we are now. So everything begins from what we want. And what is it we really want? Is there not a Great Wish behind all our petty everyday longings? There is: it is that wish to return to ourselves. We want to come back Home.

My own former deeds and wishes no doubt brought about my being born in Russia. That was in 1954. During my youth I experienced my country as a wonderland of suppression. Subjugated in every possible way, the Russian people nevertheless managed to realize something positive underneath it all: their own genuineness. A deeply Russian species of authenticity may have been the unexpected payoff for the unthinkable troubles we allowed to befall our country and ourselves. Russians became genuine amidst the muddy waters of ideological lies and political brainwashing. They became genuine, moreover, both at their worst and at their best: there was no room for superficiality.

The great sufferings visited upon the nation of course changed the people, in the structure of their consciousness as well as the patterns of their relationships. Suffering increased the tension and the density of the nation's aura, brought people closer to one another, and inevitably forced them to shift their focus inward in search of deliverance.

Historically and geographically located between the West and the East, Russia was influenced by both, absorbing, for instance, Western rationality along with Eastern approaches to metaphysical possibility. The Russian Christian Orthodox Church, with its origin in Byzantium, has not been the only tradition that had an impact on Russians. Buddhism, for instance, came from Buryatia and Tuva, and indeed the first Buddhist temple in Europe was built in St. Petersburg. Islam came from the Asian republics and Tatarstan. Judaism was preserved over the centuries by desperate Jewish communities. These together with Hinduism and yoga, shamanism and Masonic Lodges, all running alongside a great tradition of indigenous Russian mysticism and philosophy, contributed to the richness and complexity of the Russian spiritual quest.

These pages chronicle my direct experience of where that quest has most recently led us.

Tausha

The Life and Teachings of a Russian Mystic

1

Where the Darkness is at its deepest, the brightest Light shines on.

Once when I was fourteen, I stepped out of the front door of the house where I lived and was suddenly overwhelmed by the beauty of the blooming trees and the high spring sky. My being was gripped by a question: What does it all mean? That question pierced me like a lightning bolt, cutting through all my conceptions and misconceptions about existence. I looked around, amazed by the new world that had just burst open to me. This new reality had no name and could not be described. It was a partly unveiled yet still hidden mystery, with the promise of being ever-fresh and forever fathomless.

Four years later I came across a book that brought me close to an answer: *The Life of Sri Ramakrishna and The Life of Vivekananda* by Romain Rolland. Actually the sheaf of papers that I read was not a book but a pale, typewritten copy of one. It was 1972, and the book was banned because of its mystical content. In fact, most of the books I read before the collapse of the Soviet Union were typescripts or photocopies. Enthusiasts copied them for free, running the risk of being arrested for the sake of knowledge. The circumstances surrounding these handmade books resembled medieval times, but there was a positive aspect to it: severe censorship unwittingly created a unique filter through which only the best books, music, and movies could get through.

Ramakrishna and Vivekananda became my first Masters. They will be with me forever. Later came Ramana Maharshi, Yogananda, Aurobindo, Gurdjieff, and many others. Appearing on the pages as living beings, these teachers invite the reader to carry on the journey, sending their encouraging message: "There's hope on the path ahead!" So for me, Ramakrishna and Vivekananda were the first ones to point toward eternity.

For the next few years I read all the books on yoga and the occult I could lay my hands on, but reading did not change my life. It gave hope and intoxication but could not bring new dimensions of consciousness any closer. In reading I encountered a barrier like a glass wall: one could only gaze through it at beautiful, breathtaking images, but could not go beyond it.

The frustration I felt regarding the teachings only reinforced the frustration I felt as a citizen of a police state. As the years rolled on, my life ran according to the same monotonous routine so many others experienced in Soviet Society, but I for one couldn't accept it. It was like the story of an ape in the zoo, staring at two oranges placed outside its cage. One of the oranges was within reach but rotten; the other was fresh but had been placed too far away to grasp. So here were two nice options: either be satisfied with a rotten orange or stay hungry enjoying the view!

I tried to break through the glass wall—to get at the good orange— by means of meditation, but most of my lonely efforts only resulted in a sensation of strong pressure between my eyebrows, like the prelude to a headache. I was obviously barking up the wrong tree. There were a few meditation sessions, however, were I arrived at a point that I called "the screen." This screen was an enormous veil consisting of a dazzling darkness—a darkness that was yet so bright that it seemed almost blinding. The light and the darkness were one and the same, rooted deep within the same mysterious source. But the source was blocked by the screen from without and by my fear of being dissolved by it from within. I felt that any further step would require letting go of my own form, losing myself in the unknown.

In my everyday life I felt as though an endless movie consisting only of annoying dull thoughts were playing in my head, conditioning my world. I had a premonition that to change the world around me I would have to do something about that dreary film. I wasn't sure whether to stop the movie outright or just to change the footage! Besides, I did not have the slightest idea of how to accomplish either. With every bump of my head against the glass wall I abandoned myself more and more to despair.

Once I was invited to a birthday party—a typical Russian party with much talking, smoking, drinking, eating, and fooling around. I usually experienced my deepest level of depression at parties like this one. Though all my friends were having fun, I felt alienated from them and from the way they enjoyed life. A strange fantasy came to my mind: to leave the party unnoticed, head southeast (the direction from St. Petersburg, where I lived, to the Himalayan Mountains, which had attracted me like a magnet since my childhood), and to keep moving, leaving all possessions and attachments behind, just holding on to that direction.

At Russian parties people usually sit around a long table made up of a few smaller ones. I was sitting at the table languidly trying to keep up the conversation, when all of a sudden a strong urge to relax came over me in the form of an inner command.

I became so relaxed that without any effort I slipped out of the chair and found myself lying on the floor under the table, surrounded by legs and shoes. It was quiet and dark down there, and the whole outlook was so different that I thoroughly enjoyed the change in view!

Soon my disappearance was noticed and commented on in the conventional way, with everyone assuming that I had gotten loaded too soon. People started kicking me, but, as I did not show any resistance, they soon left me alone. It felt calm and secure, lying there, down in the darkness, listening to the muffled, drunken voices coming as if from some faraway place. I was growing more and more relaxed and absent, turning my focus inside, when suddenly I found myself in another world!

It was a rugged mountain landscape at dusk. Complete wilderness reigned all around. The day was cloudy and windy. I seemed to be alone in these mountains, but, turning around, I caught sight of an old man with a long gray beard whose face looked strangely familiar to me. With an inviting gesture of his hand he called to me to follow him. After a moment of hesitation I did so, and we started climbing up and down the meandering trail leading God knows where. The old man was silent and walked slowly, yet I almost had to run to keep pace with him. At last we approached a huge cave and the old man ushered me in.

There was a dim, shimmering light inside and I could distinguish a door at the other end of the hall. Without a word, the guide pointed to the door and ordered me to enter. I was frightened and upset, but an odd power emanating from the old man was taking hold of me, that I was not inclined to resist. I opened the door and entered.

Much to my surprise, I found myself back at the birthday party. The same people were there, behaving in the same way, but I realized that my attitude toward them and toward the whole situation had changed drastically. The people in the room were really my friends now. I was one of them, we loved one another, and it felt wonderful.

Suddenly I came to myself, and there I was, under the table being kicked again and being punched all over my body. Keeping my eyes closed and listening to the voices, I realized that my body was an obstacle to their moving the table to clear the room for dancing. I was capable of getting up but somehow felt unwilling to do so. My body remained deeply relaxed and numb to the thrusts and kicks it received from the angry partiers. I had apparently assumed and maintained the attitude of a dispassionate witness to all that was going on.

Failing to get me on my feet, people started blaming and insulting me in every possible way. One of them even tried to put out a cigarette on my hand, but lucky for me his girlfriend prevented him from committing this savagery. At last they dragged me out to another room, threw me down on a pile of coats, turned out the light, and left me alone.

There I was, lying in the darkness, listening detatchedly to the muffled sounds of dance music. The party was turning wild—a real wingding. I took no offence at my friends' behavior, although I no doubt had a right to. There was something mysterious, unusual about all of this. I was overcome with a queer emptiness that appeared to be both inside and outside myself. I somehow knew that my life was about to change.

The door slowly opened, and a girl I didn't know slipped in. She sat next to me and tears came to her eyes. She put her hand on my forehead and began sobbing softly, repeating, "The bastards, what have they done to you!" But pity was something I could not abide. Feeling a constriction in my throat, I jumped up, grabbed my jacket, and ran out of the house.

The next morning I resolved to fulfill my long-cherished desire to go into seclusion and pursue the contemplative life. Enough was enough. There was not much I would be leaving behind. Abandoning the pain and frustration of the big city hardly seemed a heavy price to pay in exchange for a quiet, simple life somewhere in the wilderness. The borders of the Soviet Union were closed at that time, so I would have to choose a place inside the empire. Fortunately there was plenty of room, since the USSR occupied one-sixth of the earth's surface. I decided to move to the Kamchatka Peninsula, the remotest part of Russia, to spend a few years or, perhaps the rest of my life, there as a hermit. I would need a special permit since Kamchatka is a frontier region occupied mostly by naval bases. It took me a month to get the permit and make the extra money I needed for the trip.

On the day I was to leave, as I was in fact just about to depart, the phone rang. For a number of years prior to these events I had had a presentiment about a telephone call that would change my life. This was it.

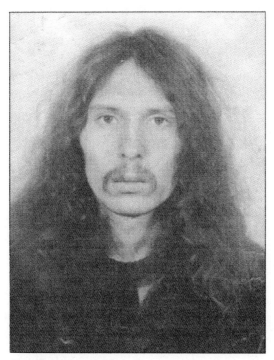

Tausha, 1980

2

We are not alone here. There are Great Ones watching over and sending out their blessing and support to all true seekers. They form the Hierarchy of Light, based on love and compassion. If you want to truly take up your place within it, you are put to the test. The test rests upon a simple question: do you have enough faith to work for the Hierarchy?

I had met the man on the phone a few times before. He was a calm, witty character, two years my junior, with long, sandy, shoulder-length hair and a steady, quiet look in his greenish eyes. I thought of him as a calligrapher and a kind of healer. He practiced "the laying on of hands," and the walls of his room were covered with strange symbols and hieroglyphic writings. A queer fish, but nothing beyond the pale. His name was Tausha.

He said that he wanted to get together and have a talk. I did not ask what it was about and just agreed to meet him at his place—a rented a room in an old part of St. Petersburg, next to Preobrajenskaya Church. The room was part of a huge communal apartment along an endless corridor shared by ten or more tenants, a typical situation for the old city.

While showing me to his room, Tausha introduced me to a tall fellow who was sitting at a table writing hieroglyphs. His name was John. Later I found out that this was a nickname given to him by Tausha because of his former sympathy for Long John Whiskey. Tausha was very good at providing nicknames. They had a tendency to become real names and stay with people forever.

"What are these hieroglyphs?" I asked, looking around. "They don't look Chinese, but they're beautiful." Pieces of paper with strange graphic symbols were all over the place.

"This is 'Set,' the sacred language of Shambhala," Tausha replied.

Of course I knew about Shambhala, the legendary Himalayan kingdom ruled by a brotherhood of immortal spiritual Masters, who protect and direct the course of earthly evolution. The messages received from there by renowned Russian mystics Madame Blavatsky and Elena Roerich were among my favorite reading.

"How do you come to know about it?" I questioned. Tausha did not answer.

"Or perhaps you've just made it up?" I continued my somewhat sarcastic interrogation.

Tausha glared at me, then smiled and said, "You may believe that, if you wish."

"What about the symbols? It's all Greek to me. Are they also from Shambhala?" I went on, with the same touch of sarcasm.

Tausha became serious and said, "No, these are symbols from Kunta yoga. It's a yoga of mystical symbols and mantras. Visualized and pronounced properly, these symbols and mantras are powerful means on the yogic path."

"Are you guys yogis?" That sounded silly even to me.

"Sort of," said Tausha abruptly, and John burst into laughter. I stared at them closely. They did not in any way fit the description of yogis. They looked like millions of other ordinary people on this planet. I decided to get down to business, but Tausha foresaw my question and asked, "Would you like to study healing?"

"What do you mean by healing?"

"I mean healing people with your hands, but with your head empty."

I laughed, "My head is already empty enough. Besides, I hate doctors. I certainly don't want to become one!"

"It has nothing to do with doctors. It has to do with Spirit."

We kept silent for a while; then I said, "I don't know. I'm about to move to Kamchatka."

Tausha gave me a piercing glance and muttered, "I doubt it." I got up, ready to leave.

"Anyway, if you decide you're interrested, let me know." He handed me a piece of paper with his telephone number written on it. Apart from the number, I noticed a few characters.

"What do these characters mean?"

"They mean: 'Do what you truly want to do.'"

3

Accept everything as it is. Don't fight the world and yourself. There is a Will behind whatever you perceive, and it's always at work without and within. Hearing these words is also the manifestation of the Will, so just surrender yourself to what is going on and find peace in the flux of events. Flow with the flux and get the feel of its wisdom.

There is only one way: down the stream, back to the ocean. Once you've stopped wasting your energy on fighting with things, you'll save it for harmony and the fulfillment of your wishes, because before reaching the ocean, every desire of yours will be fulfilled. This is the law. The law of the ocean.

If you give your will up to the Will that spins the worlds and they become one, you'll meet no obstacles—for what can hinder the Mighty itself? It's not that difficult. Just let things be as they are and watch them change. Changing is their nature and watching is your destiny. When you reach the ocean, there is no destiny any more, because the ocean is limitless. And this is freedom.

I had a couple of weeks left before my departure, and I was busy with preparations. A week passed, and I forgot about Tausha's proposal since I hadn't taken him seriously to begin with. I had met too many freaks in the course of my spiritual quest obsessed with queer ideas like "Shambhala." Madhouses in Russia were packed with such characters. Tausha and his companion seemed to be normal, but a craving for something beyond the ordinary is inherent in human nature and you never know where to draw the line between genuine inquiry and madness. But in spite of this I gave him a call. Surprisingly, considering the number of tenants in his flat, nobody answered the phone. The next day I repeated my call with the same result, then gave up, rather relieved.

My last task before making my long anticipated departure for Kamchatka was to get a detailed map of the place—not an easy task, since possessing good maps was a privilege of the military and the KGB. But I found a fellow who had served there as a border guard and owned a map, which he agreed to sell to me.

We met late at night, and by the time I had the map in my hands it was too late for the metro. I didn't have money for a taxi, so there was no choice but to walk all the way back—at least a couple of hours' journey. It might have been a nice walk if it hadn't been a zero degree December night. Walking down the snowy streets, I was trying to think of some friend's place on my way to stop at for a cup of hot tea, since there was no such thing in the Soviet Union as a late-night bar or café. At night the citizens were supposed to sleep, not eat or drink.

At last I remembered one acquaintance of mine whose place was on the way, but I was not sure if he was back from the army. I decided to give it a try anyway. After standing in his doorway pressing the buzzer for a few minutes, I accepted that my dream of a cup of hot tea was vanishing into cold thin air. Heading back down the dark stairs I heard someone open the door. I turned around and saw a figure against the light inside. It was not the owner of the apartment. It was Tausha.

"Hi," he said, without batting an eyelash. "You are right on time. Do come in."

I climbed back up and entered the apartment, feeling a bit odd as though something was just about to happen.

"How come you're here?" I asked as we sat down in the kitchen. In Russia, a kitchen is where people spend most of their time. It is the heart of the domicile. Tausha poured me a cup of tea from the boiling kettle.

"K. (Tausha named the owner of the apartment) is on a week's leave of absence from the army and left me the keys."

"He never told me that he knew you."

Tausha shrugged his shoulders. "He is the son of one of my patients."

I was enjoying the hot tea. "The telephone at your place has been dead all week. Have you moved here?"

"The line has been disconnected. I am not staying there any longer. I'll be here for a few days."

"What happened to your place? Anything wrong there?" I asked. Tausha did not answer.

"Have you decided where to live?"

"I don't know yet."

"Well, I'm leaving in a few days."

"To Kamchatka?"

"That's right. Have you been there?"

"No. I've heard it's a beautiful place."

"Oh, yes. Volcanoes, geysers..."

We remained silent for a while, then I got up, intending to leave. "Okay, thanks for the tea. I must be going. It's an hour's walk to my place from here."

Tausha looked at me inquisitively, scanning me from head to toe.

"Wait a minute. I'd like to ask you something."

"Go ahead."

"Would you like me to be your boss?"

I didn't get it. "What?"

"Do you want to me to be your leader?"

I was really taken aback by such a self-confident demand.

"My leader... in what?"

"In everything."

"Like...like the Heavenly Father?"

"Exactly." Tausha smiled and pointed his finger at the ceiling. I put on my thinking cap.

"You mean do I want to obey you like a dog?"

"Yes, if you want to put it that way. Anyway, you'd be required to follow my instructions."

It was a spectacular offer. I gazed at Tausha, trying to figure him out. He did not look particularly obnoxious. He was quiet and relaxed, scrutinizing me with his deep greenish eyes. It was like a staring duel. At last I said, "You must be kidding."

"Not in the least. I'm quite serious."

I had no idea what to say. *He must be nuts!* flashed in the back of my mind. But the conversation was taking an undeniably interesting turn, and I chose to play along.

"All right, if I say 'yes,' what will happen to me?"

"We'll get to that point only after you do it."

"Tricky enough. And if I don't buy it?"

"Then you are free to follow your way. Just take it or leave it."

"Am I supposed to give you my answer now?"

Tausha took a look at his watch. "Tonight, anyhow."

I still could not make out if he was putting me on. "Okay. Let's say I have agreed, but I do not follow your instructions at all. What are you going to do then?"

Tausha said with a smile, "That is not going to happen."

"Why?"

"Simply because once you say 'yes' you will not be able to act differently."

I somehow realized that he was right. But I did not *think* it. My body *sensed* it was true. It was my first experience of the language of the body, the only language that cannot lie. I knew once I said yes, that was it. My body told me there was no turning back. It made my flesh creep.

4

If you meet the Teacher, it doesn't mean that you'll recognize him; if you recognize him, it doesn't mean that you're ready to learn; if you're ready to learn, it doesn't mean that you're ready to surrender; if you're ready to surrender, you don't need a teacher.

The doorbell gave a particular series of rings, like a code. I wondered who might be arriving at 2 a.m. Tausha opened the door, and from where I was sitting I could see the night guest coming in. I was astonished at what I saw—a woman in her forties, the very stereotype of a witch: ugly, slim, with a huge nose, black hair and dark sparkling eyes, exquisitely dressed. Her name was Nana. She was a Gypsy. Tausha introduced me as a chum of his. She had brought some delicacies, and, as she informed Tausha about some current events of concern to them both, she began to lay her fare out on the table. Nana invited me to join the meal. I declined.

Watching them eating and talking, I got really scared. They were discussing the research work of a KGB parapsychology laboratory which presumably intended to get Tausha involved in their experiments. In those days, the very mention of the KGB awakened extreme caution in the Russian heart. It is no exaggeration to say that the Soviet secret police had become a veritable earthly embodiment of evil. Over sixty million citizens had been exterminated by it. There was no family in Russia that had not lost at least one member to its repression. Typically, KGB agents would arrive at night in a black car, knock on the door, seize the head of the family and make away with him. Once taken, he was gone forever. The best part of the nation, the cream of the population, had been eliminated. The best farmers, the shrewdest intellectuals, writers, doctors, whoever. At one time, almost the entire cultural, philosophical, military elite had been eliminated, but so had innumerable ordinary citizens.

Yet it was not only the topic of KGB purges that scared me now; there was something more to my fear. Perhaps due to the physical appearance of the woman or to Tausha's imponderable proposal or just because of the increasingly eerie nighttime atmosphere, I felt myself being pulled into a fiendish enterprise that I was *almost* certain it would be better to avoid. On the other hand, something was holding me, drawing me, attracting me, and it was not about to let me go.

I ended up walking out of the kitchen and lying down on the sofa in the dining room, attempting to pull myself together. Intuitively I felt that Tausha was right. To gain something, first you have to give something. But he demanded my whole self, without giving me a chance to check him out beforehand. I can't say I valued my own personality all that much, but, like they say, discretion is the better part of valor. So I resolved to put him to the test. The problem was that I didn't have the slightest idea what kind of a test would satisfy my doubts.

Then I recalled, in a kind of reverie, an old Hindu legend that goes something like this:

> *Once upon a time, there was a woman in India named Lakshmi who became a widow. According to the ancient Indian custom called* suttee, *a widow was supposed to commit suicide by throwing herself on her husband's funeral pyre. If she refused to do so, she would be ostracized for the rest of her days. She would be an outcast and would have to live apart from people. That was just what happened to Lakshmi. She refused to submit to suttee, not because she feared agonizing death, but because she had already resolved to pursue the ultimate wish of her heart: to find the Divine Guru. The nobility of that wish enabled her to sustain public disgrace.*
>
> *Lakshmi found a deserted shack alongside a wide road and settled down there. People from all walks of life moved along the road, among them pilgrims and the wandering ascetics called* sadhus. *Lakshmi sat by the door of her shack watching those sadhus pass by, in hope that someday her Gurudeva would show up and satisfy her quest for the Divine.*
>
> *There was a generous Indian custom of feeding the wandering sadhus by putting food on a shelf outside the house in the evening so that they could pick it up early in the morning undisturbed and proceed on their way. As time elapsed, Lakshmi continued to share her scarce food with wandering truth seekers. She had decided that when the time came that she recognized her real guru, she would put poisonous*

food on the shelf to verify his authenticity. The years were passing by, yet the guru had failed to appear. Never did Lakshmi's heart tell her to put someone to the test.

But finally a morning came when she saw an approaching sadhu, and her heart said that he was the one. Lakshmi promptly placed some poisonous rice and fruits on the shelf and hid herself inside the shack, peering out through a tiny window. The sadhu ate the poisonous meal, recited a mantra and walked on, intact.

Catching up with him, Lakshmi knelt down, imploring the sadhu to accept her as a disciple. He turned back and said that as she had neglected the sacrificial custom of suttee he could not accept her. Crying, Lakshmi asked the sadhu what she could do to atone her guilt. "Make a fire and perform your duty," was the answer. Inspired by the fact that she had found the long-awaited guru, Lakshmi obeyed. She made a huge bonfire behind the house and ran into it. But the fire didn't burn her and died away.

"Now you can follow me," were the words of the sadhu. They moved on and the road soon consumed them.

When I came back to the kitchen, Nana was about to leave. I noticed that the fear stimulated by her appearance had gone, and that she did not look so ugly after all.

"It was a pleasure to meet you," I told her.

"All the best to you. I hope we'll meet again soon," she said, winking at me.

By the time Nana left, I knew what the test was going to be.

5

Search for fear, for it marks the boundary of your petty self. Wherever you find it, you stand on the verge of discovering a new land.

I sat down by Tausha's side to resume the conversation we had begun before Nana's arrival. "I would like you to explain to me a certain phenomenon I experienced about eight years ago. Perhaps you can shed some light on it for me. So far nobody has been able to."

Tausha nodded.

"When I was eighteen, I was at a friend's apartment—just a small room with carpets hung on the walls. It was a little after midnight. We were sitting in armchairs facing each other, with a window to our right. Outside the window, a street lantern swung in the fall wind.

"Both of us wrote poetry at the time, and we liked to recite it and talk about literature. My friend recited some verses by Baratynsky, one of our finest poets. The verses were so profound that there was nothing left to say, and quite naturally we sank into silence. I don't know for how long we remained there, immersed in a sort of poetic trance, but all of a sudden I felt that there was somebody besides the two of us, in the room.

"I raised my eyes, and what I saw standing by the window I will never forget until the day I die. It was the most terrifying and sinister creature I had ever encountered—a male, about eight feet tall, wearing a long dark mantle, with an absolutely bald head and disproportionately long ears. His skin was grayish white, and he was grinning silently with a leer of the utmost contempt and hauteur. He did not *belong* there. He *was* there, but at the same time, he wasn't. I could see him in minute detail, although I did not see him with my physical eyes. It was another form of vision that I have since come to think of as 'mental vision.'

"With this kind of vision, it seems, one can see objects belonging to another dimension that penetrates ours, or, perhaps, is parallel to it. Under usual circumstances, obviously, we're unable to perceive this dimension, but if our focus shifts in a certain way, or an object from it reaches "critical mass" and breaks through onto our level of perception, we become aware of it. So I beheld this being as if my brain had been ripped open and I was looking from the inside out.

"The vision itself was not as bad as the freezing that blew from the creature's presence. It had a paralyzing impact on my body, and its power was overwhelming. My muscles became numb, including my vocal cords, so that I could not even scream—my throat was frozen, like after being given a local anesthetic. The only sound I managed to utter was a weak wheeze.

"Somehow, the wind did not affect my eye muscles, and my eyes were my only bodily parts that I remained in control of. I looked at my friend, and by his deadly pale, distorted face I could see that he was being put through the same ordeal."

I interrupted my narration, for I noticed that Tausha seemed to have dirfted off somewhere. His eyes were half closed, as if he were taking a nap. "Are you dozing off?" I asked.

"Certainly not. Please go on."

I continued, but as I spoke, it was as if the words were forming by themselves. I said, "I don't remember how long my paralytic stupor lasted. Eventually the being passed through the window and took his stance outside under the street lamp some yards away. Our world of matter was apparently insubstantial for him, and he easily moved through solid objects. But even more strange was that I was able to perceive him standing there right through the wall!

"His ice-like, paralyzing energy field did not work at such a distance, however; so, having recuperated a bit, we regained our ability to move, though we still were unable to utter a sound. As the hypnotic effect of his presence continued to abate, we began making odd mumbling noises and making senseless gestures. The monster was still there under the street lamp, watching us with that same contemptuous leer.

"Eventually we started talking, more or less coherently. I recall myself saying something like, 'Remember him standing in here?' But as soon as I said this, the devilish creature stepped back into the room and took the same position by the window he had occupied before. We became hypnotized again, like rabbits in front of a snake.

"Then my mind went blank, and the next thing I remember is dashing out of the apartment and down the street alone with my teeth chattering loudly in the night. Before this experience, whenever I'd read about the phenomenon of chattering teeth, I thought it was a poetical metaphor. It is not. I was unable to make my teeth stop even when I got home and was snug in my bed.

"My friend also was unable to stay at his place that night. He too ran away and slept somewhere else.

"Since that night, a deep apprehension that this being might return has settled in my heart. It is not a fear for my life or sanity; it has more to do with a discouraging awareness of my weakness and helplessness before him, because his power is too alien, somehow too 'far off' to control. Sometimes, just by bringing the thought of him to mind, I immediately feel the same disgusting cold vibration in my heart and have to make an effort to shift the focus of my attention onto something else, in fear that if I didn't, he'd appear."

Tausha interrupted me, "Do you feel it now?"

"Yes, I do, a little bit. Why?"

He did not answer. "Go on."

"I've been feeling this being lurking at the margins of my consciousness all these years; I know he is still out there, perhaps waiting for another chance to come.

"That's the story. Can you tell me what this was all about and what I ought to do to get rid of my fear?"

Tausha remained silent for a while; then he leaned back in his chair and said affirmatively, as if he had been dealing with things like this on a daily basis, "These creatures were angels before Satan's revolt, but after that pitiable event, as the Bible says, one third of them fell along with their Chief. This particular one was a demon," said Tausha, squinting his eyes, "of the eighth degree."

"But what did he come for?"

Tausha grinned. "To introduce himself. And to expand your knowledge." Then he added seriously, "He was attracted by something in you."

"You mentioned his 'degree.' What's that about?"

"There is an old classification of demonic ranks and energy levels. It really should be modernized. The demons of the eighth degree are able to cause the paralyzing sensation you experienced."

"Can they cause death?"

"Sometimes, but in most cases death is only caused by the demons of the ninth degree and higher."

"How many degrees are there?"

"Twelve—of the Dark Hierarchy. The Forces of Light have only eleven. The twelve disciples of Jesus were supposed to 'cover' twelve levels of Darkness, but since the Judas treachery the twelfth level has remained uncovered."

"Is it for that reason that we face so much evil on earth today?"

"Partly. In the Christian countries, at least. But let's get back to your story. You asked me how you might eliminate your fear. There is only one way to do it—eliminate the demon itself."

"But that's impossible. You underestimate his power. If we summon him, we'll just be blown away."

"Relax. Dealing with what you call his 'power' is my job. But I'll need your consent."

I grew pensive. I did not expect that my test would go so far as to risk an actual encounter with the thing. I just wanted Tausha to give me a reasonable explanation, that was all. But to deal with the monster again? He just didn't realize what kind of mortal danger he was going to expose us to. On the other hand, it was a real chance to check Tausha out, whatever the cost might be, and, perhaps, to get rid of my fear.

"All right, I agree. What must I to do?"

"Call him."

"How?"

"Focus on him and call him in."

It was not difficult, as I had been used to visually imagining his bald head and weird ears for many years, as well as feeling his cold presence whenever I told the story.

The demon fell into our space and took shape right away. The door of the room was open and I saw him standing there, about fifteen feet away.

Tausha spotted the demon too, for he turned in his direction, put his hands on his knees and concentrated. I knew that at such a distance the paralyzing aura of the demon did not work, but if he moved closer... the thought started a wave of terror rolling through me.

As if attracted by my panic, the demon began coming toward us. At that moment I heard Tausha gnashing his teeth. I was ready for the worst. Ten feet away, the creature suddenly came to a halt, as if having run into an invisible barrier. Tausha's energy was blocking the demon. I could feel it with my whole body. Tausha had set up an energy circle that the monster was unable to break into. This circle was intense but elastic. It pushed the demon back as if it were a rubber pad.

"He can't come in. You're blocking him off!"

"Draw him in," Tausha commanded.

I tried to pull the demon inside the circle, but he seemed reluctant to move. All of a sudden Tausha flung out his hands with the fingers stretched forward. One hand pointed at the demon, the other at myself. At the same moment I felt myself being penetrated by a powerful energetic impulse that shot through me like a flash. Then there was a shriek—the most disgusting and horrendous sound I have ever heard. Shrill and long, it might have belonged to a mortally wounded pterodactyl. I heard the shriek clearly, but not with my physical ears. It sounded in my inner hearing just as the demon appeared to my mental vision.

Tausha lowered his hands. "We've zapped him," he said, "but check it out for yourself. I may have only cut the channel. Focus on him again."

I did, and to my great relief, I felt neither the cold vibration nor the fear. All that came up was an ordinary memory, a single image without any power.

"I can't find him," I said affirmatively.

"And you won't. It's over."

"What happened to him? Is he dead?"

"Let's put it this way. He doesn't exist."

"Why did you thrust out your hands that way you did?"

"I sent an energy ray through you that burned him down."

"Why through me?"

"Because it was your connection. You had a channel to him."

"And what did you do with the other hand?"

"It was a trap. I drew him into it and just didn't let him go."

"Why were you gnashing your teeth?"

Tausha looked at me in surprise, "I wasn't."

"But I heard it," I insisted. For a moment it seemed like he didn't know what I was talking about, but in an instant he regained his poise, as if he himself were coming to a recognition of something.

"It was just his last trick. He tried to fool you. Any more questions?"

"No."

Tausha sank into silence. I was glad to have some time to take it all in.

6

The more you give, the more you are given. In giving you liken yourself to God, who is the Giver, and His light comes upon you.

With his long sandy hair and light red mustache, Tausha definitely did not look like a "spiritual teacher." If I met him on the street, I would have taken him for an artist or a poet. But there was something about Tausha that was beyond my comprehension; his response to my "test" was so masterful and competent, that I knew I couldn't just walk away from him.

I looked up and glanced at him. Tausha was relaxed and quiet, with his eyes focused on my person, but not looking into my eyes. It was as if he were gazing at something invisible inside me. He was performing some inner action I had never observed anyone perform before, and that action held my fascination. I could sense with my whole body that he was *doing* something to or with me—something tranquil yet so intense that I could feel the air around him growing *dense*.

I had always thought of work on one's consciousness as immeasurably superior to any effort aimed at mere external achievement. Such work was what I was going to Kamchatka for. I assumed it had nothing to do with the thinking process or meditation (in the sense of closing one's eyes and waiting for something beautiful to manifest); I thought it should simply involve adopting another way of life. But here was Tausha, sitting in front of me, focused on something I couldn't see. I had contrived a test of his power, and he had passed it beyond my wildest expectation. But I still wasn't sure I was ready to commit my spiritual future to him.

Suddenly Tausha broke the silence. "Fighting demons is not what I'm here for. My task is to expand the network of Light that has been created, developed and preserved through the ages by the Forces of Light for the purpose of distributing energy. This network is the blood of great souls, shed for our salvation, and we are truly alive once we feed on it.

"We must create a new mesh of this Light here, in St. Petersburg. If we succeed, it will be just a beginning. You might say we have to put our best foot forward."

I was amazed. It was as if he was responding to my unasked question.

I asked, "How do we do that? How does this mesh work?"

"On an energetic level, it works like a whirlpool that pulls energy in and causes it to spin around with it. The stronger the whirlpool is, the more people get involved in the structure. The energy circulating inside the mesh has an impact on the timing of both individual and general evolution. Energy is the fuel of evolution, and every true spiritual practice is nothing but an acceleration of the evolutionary process. Practice can render tens or even hundreds of painful incarnations unnecessary. The core of any real spiritual practice is fighting time!

"On the other hand, energy is not the only thing we need. Wisdom is required as well. We have to know what to do with our power, lest it express itself in a destructive way.

"Where does this wisdom come from," I asked.

"To get the whole process started, there has to be a blessing—an active connection with a higher source. The blessing often takes the form of a shaft of pale green light shining down onto the mesh. We are not working alone here, and every true evolutionary effort earns a response. The Sufi masters call this greenish beam *baraka*, which means *grace*, or the *power given for the work.*

"If you are granted the blessing of this shaft of light, what is required of you is service. This service is not abject subservience; it is the difficult process of becoming a channel, a link connecting the realm of the high energies to this world. The more you become open to the shaft of light (and this means the more you open yourself to its source), the more sacrifice is required. The best channel is an empty one. So you must work at dissolving yourself until you realize that you are just another wave in the ocean of consciousness."

Emboldened by what felt like a rush of the very energy he was talking about, I dared to voice what remained a lurking doubt. "How can I make sure that you are not serving the Devil?"

Tausha laughed, but my heart was in my mouth.

"Good question. Whatever I say, you won't believe me until you figure it out for yourself. It's too considerable a subject to get into right now. Better leave the Prince of the World alone for a while."

I must have had an expression of disbelief, for Tausha added, "Just leave it like this: you don't know who I am or who is standing behind me. So what? You have a chance to find out."

I was at a loss to know how to react to that. Tausha seemed to be a very different kind of teacher from those I had read about. I sighed, without feeling much relief, and asked, "Suppose I accept you as my 'boss'—was that the way you put it?"

Tausha nodded ironically.

"What would be your first instruction for me to follow?"

Tausha was ready with the answer. "I want you to practice Disa."

"Disa?"

"It's a simple thing—a principle of behavior: *Do only what you really want to.*"

I laughed. "But this is impossible!"

"It is possible, if you've got the guts."

"But if we could do whatever we want, it would mean that we were free. But unfortunately, we are not."

"Do you enjoy thinking this way?" Tausha grinned.

"It's just the way it is, whether I like it or not," I said affirmatively.

"But how do you like the fact that we have free will, which is our birthright?"

"Sure, but..."

"No 'buts'," Tausha interrupted me. "We are free to do what we want, and for most of us it is the only freedom we have. Get a taste of it."

"Well, we've got certain responsibilities and obligations." Immediately I myself felt that my remark was off the mark.

"There are no responsibilities except those you've taken on yourself, right?"

"True, but I have to work to earn my living."

"No, you don't. To be exact, you can if you want to, but that is not a necessity. There is another type of work you can be paid for."

"Where do you expect the money to come from?"

Tausha smiled and pointed his index finger toward the ceiling. "From up there."

"A celestial bank account?" I quipped.

"The Disa fund," he corrected me.

I conceded, "Well, I admit that you might be able to attract money through your, so to speak, special abilities, but be sure the world is going to become a slaughterhouse if people fly off the handle practicing Disa."

"Or a paradise. You mistake Disa for wantonness, but actually it is a meditative approach, requiring perfect sincerity and self-control. If you deviate from your sincerity, you lose Disa. But in any case, Disa is an esoteric practice, and I'm not about to offer it to the general public."

"Okay. But let's say I make an attempt to kill you right now."

"Is that what you really want to do?"

"No, but..."

"Then killing me is not Disa. Actually, what you really do want right now is to take a pee," he said banteringly.

I laughed. "Right," and I got up and went to the bathroom.

When I returned, Tausha continued, "You are free to kill me, but I'm also free to defend myself, to give up, or to act any way I like."

"What's the difference, then, between a Disa behavior and a normal one?"

"Normally, people are programmed and act according to their actions in the past and by the limitations imposed on them by the world."

"This is called karma, isn't it?"

"Correct."

"So, is Disa a kind of reprogramming?"

"I'd rather say a de-programming. A desire is a basic thing, an integral part of ourselves, following us through existence. So why not start with the basics? There is a spiritual law that says that we exist as individuals until we have fulfilled all our wishes. But Disa is not wishful thinking. It is an investigation of desires.

"Practiced in sincerity, Disa leads to one of two realizations. With the first realization you understand that you cannot be satisfied with your petty desires anymore. You come to realize that there is only one great Wish living in your heart, the king of wishes—your longing for Realization. All other desires become subordinate to this main one, and your life changes as a consequence.

"The other possible realization is that, as a matter of fact, you do not really want anything. Your little 'I' doesn't exist as a reality at all. And your big 'I' is content with itself, inasmuch as it includes everything."

There was a silence, broken at length by my question, "And if Disa is done in the wrong way?"

"If done in the wrong way, Disa can be destructive and danger-ous."

"What are the main hindrances on this path?"

"Disa lets you see your fears right away and makes you deal with them."

"What should I do to overcome my fears?"

"Go on with Disa."

"But often we just don't know what we want. What should we do then?"

"Follow the first impulse. The first impulse is always correct."

As I asked these questions and took in Tausha's responses, all along a singular process was occurring inside me. I was attempting to locate my inner wishes. I was beginning to practice Disa. I asked out loud, "What do I want right now? I want you to show me your healing technique."

"No problem. Go and lie down on the carpet."

I followed Tausha's instruction.

The thought came to me, "This is what I want—just to stretch out and relax."

Tausha sat down cross-legged behind me and touched my temples lightly with his palms. Feeling nothing in the beginning, I was drop-ping off to sleep when there came an airy tingling inside my head. Soon this sensation spread all over, gradually turning into an over-whelming wave of dazzling energy, penetrating every cell of my body. I gave in to the wave and was swept away.

I felt propelled into a level of trance where my sense of reality seemed unbounded by time and space. I was in a world of molten gold. Forever changing, constantly in motion, that golden world was nothing but a pure shining consciousness, spreading into infinity, and its essence was joy.

There were beings living in this glowing, open space. Their glitter-ing bodies did not have a solid shape. They were flowing and chang-ing, interweaving and interacting with one another as well as with the space in, around, and between them, which consisted of the same golden consciousness.

This place was "home," and experiencing it was worth anything and everything. All the pain and frustration of countless incarnations was compensated for a million-fold. I realized that all my endeavors in life subconsciously had had only one purpose: getting to this place.

There seemed to be no other sense to earthly life.

While coming to myself I heard my voice uttering as if from far away, "Home, that's home."

When I opened my eyes I saw Tausha sitting in the armchair smiling. "Welcome back."

I was in this world again, and desperately rubbed my eyes, "No. I want to be back there."

"One swallow doesn't make a summer. The time hasn't come yet. We've got work to do."

7

There was a man called Nami who once had a dream. In this dream he saw an unknown, faraway city. There was a certain man living in this city, and in the basement of his house there was a buried treasure that, though he owned the house, he was not aware of.

Waking in the morning, Nami went to the marketplace and began asking the merchants about the city he had seen in his dream, but nobody had ever heard of such a place. At last he came across a trader who recognized his description of the city. He had visited this place with his caravan and knew how to get there. It was a long way off.

The next day Nami set off for the city, and in a month's time reached his destination. He found the house and knocked on the door. The host turned out to be a hospitable person, and finding that Nami was a stranger, invited him in for dinner. During the meal, Nami could not help scheming how to lure the man out of the house so that he could get at the treasure. While Nami was scheming, the host began to tell Nami about a dream that he had recently dreamed, in which he saw a great treasure buried in the basement of a house in a faraway city. From the description of the house, to his astonishment, Nami realized that it was his own!

The next morning, Nami set off for home. Upon his arrival, he went down to his basement, took a shovel, and dug up an immeasurable treasure.

We sat up the rest of the night, and I left early in the morning. It was a dark, cold weekday. Sullen people were lining up at the bus stops desperately trying to jam themselves into the already overcrowded buses. There was not even a glimmer of hope in their faces. The dim horizon was sheathed with vapors from smokestacks. The city seemed to be filled with gloom. Another day in the Soviet hell had begun.

It was the city where I had spent my whole life, yet now I perceived it in quite a different way. Everything seemed unreal to me. All these cars, buildings, and desolate people were nothing but the ghostly props and weary actors in a play by an unspired playwright. Exhausted, anxious, these programmed zombies had betrayed the very essence of their being—evershining joy. They were substituting for it with a grinding routine they mistook for the way life had to be.

The more I looked into the faces of my compatriots, the more I saw how far they were from the existence they had been created for, and how they were being compelled to do things they actually hated. Who was there to blame for it but themselves?

Though I hadn't given Tausha my "yes" that night, he would never ask me for it. I knew that my life had taken a new course, and that at last I had found the man who would give me the knowledge that, a few hours earlier, I was about to seek in the Kamchatka woods. If only I could partake of what he had to offer.

The next day I returned my ticket and invited Tausha to move in with me. I had a big, two-bedroom state apartment, previously occupied by my friend Felix's sister and her family. They had emigrated to Israel a few months earlier. Felix had given me the keys. Things were so inscrutable regarding lodgings under the Soviet regime, that I knew we could be forced to leave at any time, but it was just as likely that several rent-free years would pass without even an inquiry. This was a normal state of affairs in the Soviet Union of 1980.

Once Tausha moved in, I could see that he was a man of few wants. Tausha had no possessions except for a few unfinished manuscripts, a bundle of papers covered with hieroglyphs, and some watercolors. His daily routine was unconventional: he went to bed in the morning at about 8 a.m. and got up sometime around noon. I asked him about his strange schedule. Tausha replied that the energy field of the city was clearer at night, and that therefore it was easier for him to "work" at that time.

I realized from the very first day we settled down together what kind of work it was. Tausha was changing the energy structure of space itself, deploying the same overwhelming power that had drawn me into the world of molten gold. Gradually the apartment was turning into a kind of a high-voltage fishbowl; before long the energy became so intense that four hours of sleep was quite enough, not only for Tausha, but for anyone living there. With Tausha working in the apartment, the outside world did not seem to have much importance or even reality, so I stayed inside practically all the time.

I became aware that this incredible energy did not belong to Tausha *per se*. Indeed, he was working as a channel, driven by something totally beyond my comprehension. At times the current flushing through him became so powerful that I actually felt myself being subjected to something like a great wind and had to hold onto my chair. Sometimes I would pinch myself as a reality check, for my body itself did not seem solid anymore. There was no pain at all, but I knew this was no dream. It was as if my fleshly state had come to an end, and I would exclaim, aghast, "What are you doing to me?" Most of the time Tausha just smiled in reply.

It was not easy in the beginning to come to terms with my suspicion that the fellow was possessed. My nimble imagination continually fantasized horrible results to the work, like my being transmuted into a kind of zombie, will-deprived, ready to carry out any deranged orders. Tausha did not try to dissuade me from these self-inflicted terrors. In fact I think he had a lot of fun watching me being scared.

Before long I discovered that it was impossible to learn very much about the work without surrendering myself. I tended to listen suspiciously to what Tausha had to say, but I began to see that any hint of doubt regarding the energy flow itself would shut the doors to its perception. True listening took place only when I was neither anticipating nor judging. So there was nothing to do but intentionally fight the doubt. Years later I would find out that the people in close contact with Tausha who did not overcome their distrust gained very little benefit in terms of spiritual understanding. This understanding is really a strange thing, for it can hardly be conveyed in words. I often found myself just sitting silently by Tausha's side like a cat, soaking up knowledge that to this day I cannot verbalize. Wisdom flowed from heart to heart through the experience of inner stillness.

Tausha used to say, "Understanding means action." If we say "I understand" but our deeds remain unchanged, it is just a mental comprehension. True understanding is inevitably followed by right action.

8

Not what—but how!

For the first few days (or nights, to be exact), along with sessions of energy transformation, Tausha gave me some formal training in Kunta yoga.

Kunta yoga, a branch of Agni yoga, is the yoga of mystical symbols and mantras. This system was developed by the yogi Maharama Kunta and his four disciples in the second century A.D. Kunta Yoga has been preserved since that time, and Tausha is only the second man in the modern era to have accessed it. The first one was the famous Russian artist, Kazimir Malevitch, who reproduced certain Kunta yoga symbols in his Supremacist paintings of the twenties.

The symbols of Kunta are presented as graphic glyphs. The form of each symbol resonates with a specific set of astral vibrations and in fact creates them when gazed at, visualized, or drawn. When meditating on the glyphs in a certain sequence, one comes into resonance with Shakti, the creative energy of the cosmos, in a specific way, and for the specific purpose of that sequence. Below, for example, is the protective symbol "IM." When visualized inside the body, IM protects you from any kind of danger. Pronounced simultaneously with the visualization, this mantra enhances the desired effect.

Kunta comprises hundreds of symbols. Visualized inside the chakras or nadis (energy centers and channels), they bring internal purification and energy. They can also be used for controlling or changing external situations by affecting the patterns that underly them. For example, an attack can be neutralized by visualizing a particular symbol directly between the attacker and the victim. Here is this symbol—"AHIMSA":

There is a variety of general symbols for purification, energizing, harmonizing, protection, etc., along with more specific ones for performing various tasks such as finding your soul mate, establishing a connection with the sun and the moon, sending a manifestation of evil or violence back to its source, healing yourself or others, and so on.

The secret of the practice is to visualize the symbols vividly, first with eyes closed and, eventually, with eyes open, projecting the symbol into external space. Being seen in this way, they transform the energies of the space or of the body in which they are visualized, bringing about the desirable results. The following symbol is "HIAL." It is used to recharge oneself with fresh new energy. The word HIAL is a mantra.

Most of the symbols are accompanied by mantras. Chanted skillfully, the mantra induces a special, high-pitched, rustling sound, unrelated to the chanter, which remains audible as an aftereffect. Once this sound is evoked, the mantra, combined with the corresponding visualization, reaches the zenith of its power.

The Kunta yoga teaching also involves the positioning of hands and fingers for meditation purposes (mudra), breathing exercises (pranayama), and some calligraphy for the proper drawing of the symbols. The following symbol is called "SUN CROSS." It strengthens one's connection with the energy of the sun.

Drawing the symbols came easy to me since I was an artist by profession, but visualizing them as well as pronouncing the mantras correctly was much more difficult. There was no problem in seeing the symbols with my eyes closed, but to behold them in external space took several weeks of practice.

On the second night of our nocturnal life together, I asked Tausha about his plans. He answered with a question. "Do you feel the energy flow coming down all the time?"

"I do."

"Do you think it is something that is being *given* to us?"

"Certainly."

"What do you suppose it's given for?"

"For transformation, I guess..."

"For whose transformation?"

I began to realize what he meant. "The flow has to be passed on, right?"

"Exactly."

"Do you have people to pass it on to?"

"I've got a few, but there must be many more. That's the demand of the flow. If you keep it to yourself, it ceases. There are great changes coming in this country and it's part of our task to speed up this process." Tausha picked up a cigarette pack that was lying on the table and handed it to me. It was a pack of "Cosmos," Soviet cigarettes.

"Look at the picture."

The pack was dark blue. In the lower left-hand corner was a red, five-pointed star releasing something that actually looked like a white trident, though it was supposed to represent a spaceship. Suddenly the hidden meaning of the design struck me.

Tausha smiled. "You got it! The red star, struck by a white trident. Quite an anti-Soviet picture, don't you think?"

I laughed, "The designer would end up in jail, if the authorities guessed."

"You bet. It's just a little thing, but it reflects the tendency."

The year was 1980, and at that time there was no end to the Communist dictatorship in sight. I gazed at Tausha incredulously. "Do you believe that somehow *we* might bring down the regime? We're not going to meddle with politics, are we?"

"No. We're just plowing the soil. We are to work with people's consciousness, but it inevitably will have an impact on the social structure."

"How about the KGB?"

"We have some people working there, and I hope there will be more."

"You mean Nana?"

"She's not the only one. Besides, don't forget," Tausha repeated his gesture of pointing to the ceiling, "we're protected. But anyway, you should be ready for anything."

"For example?"

"For example, India."

"Are we going to India?"

Tausha laughed, "No, that's what the special prison barracks for believers and mystics is called in jailhouse slang. It has a concrete floor covered with water which naturally turns into ice in wintertime. The prisoners are forced to squat on long poles suspended over the water, praying and meditating—those, anyway, who still can. If somebody falls down, the others raise him up and tie him to the pole so he won't fall again. Dandaron, the prominent Buddhist master who was murdered in a Soviet concentration camp, had been confined in such a place."

I couldn't help interjecting, "Why do spiritually evolved people get killed or persecuted so often?"

"Because the higher vibrations do activate the Dark Forces."

"So what's the plan?"

Tausha was silent for a while, then he gave me a pin-sharp look and said, "I am a healer, and I know that of all the ways of influencing people, healing with energy brings about the most intimate and drastic impact on human consciousness. If you are able to help people with your hands, you don't need words to persuade them. My plan is to train a group of spiritual healers so that they can spread the teaching through their work and build up a network of such groups around the country. These groups might work out other practices as well, but I see healing as the basic thing."

"Why do you think that healers who are just being trained will be able to form such a network? It seems to me that this kind of work requires a great deal of energy."

"The energy is unlimited. It is being given freely—you yourself feel it already. The possibility has opened up just recently for the kind of work we're talking about. The dimesnion of the flow is widening, therefore it finds more receivers. It moves along like a chain reaction. The time is ripe, and the Light is ready to break through."

"All right. If the energy is there, then what's the problem?"

"People. The right people."

9

Prayer is talking to God; meditation is listening to Him.
After you pray, be still and listen.

When I retired to my room and went to bed after our conversation, I fell asleep right away. I have noticed generally that, when the flow is moving intensely, I experience a certain subtle form of fatigue as though the cells of my body had been slightly burned from inside and needed some rest. This is what was happening now.

After I had been asleep for some time, a silver-white, shimmering light broke my slumber. The source of the light was not in my room. It glimmered through the wall separating my room from Tausha's, and I was about to get up and go there, when the gentle touch of what seemed like a powerful, disembodied *will* restrained me. I obeyed and stayed in bed. In response to my obedience, the light intensified and enshrouded my body with a new vibration, whose sublime clarity transcended all I had experienced so far. There was something deeply personal in this light, as if I myself were the being dearest to it, even the only one it touched in this way. Suddenly I felt like I was flying, supported by the mighty hands of the light.

I don't know how long I'd been in this state when Tausha burst into the room. His eyes were wide open, and I realized that something extremely serious was going on.

"Do you realize who just came in here?" he exclaimed, breathlessly.

"No."

"Jesus Christ himself!"

I sat straight up. "Just before you came in, I did experience the presence of a powerful light," I reported.

"It was His light. I saw Him just as I am seeing you, even clearer."

"What did he look like?"

"At first I was meditating, then all of a sudden I saw His face. The light of His eyes was so dazzling, I almost couldn't stand it. Then I found myself in an endless luminous space where I saw His figure. It was only Him and me, nothing else, standing in a shoreless void. The earth and all its tragedies and sorrows seemed far away, lost somewhere in the boundless cosmos.

"Jesus looked nothing like his popular image—nothing you would find on a Christmas card. He was much more severe. Not a drop of sweetness, but the austere and martial demeanor of a warrior."

"Did you talk?"

"Yes, but without words. I asked Him for a blessing for the work. He said it was not going to be the way I expect it to be, and that if we entered the path of service, there was no turning back to the selfish way of life. He warned me that we have approached the point of no return. If we continue, we don't belong to ourselves anymore. We'll be given so much energy that it will destroy us if we back out. This is the law of the Father."

"Did He give His blessing?"

"He asked me whether I still wanted it. I said yes, and He raised His hands, palms open toward me. Then He stepped backwards and seemed to enter a kind of white wall, and His image became imprinted upon it. The image was flat, in black and white, like a charcoal drawing. I turned toward the image, raised my hands the same way He had, and spontaneously sent out into the infinite shining space the incantation: 'Power of Light, come upon us, stay with us, let us be faithful to you.'

"Then I found myself back in the room lying on the bed. The room was still shimmering with light, and, to my bewilderment, I was not alone! Someone completely unknown to me was sitting in the armchair.

"'Who are you?' I asked him telepathically. The stranger stood up and approached me. He was a tall man in his forties with a beard and deep eyes. 'You need a doctor,' he said. 'What?' I thought, 'I'm a doctor myself!'

"'You need a doctor,' he repeated, and placed his hand over my eyes. Suddenly, it was as if a veil fell from my vision, and I saw my body from the *inside*. I perceived it on the energetic and the physical levels simultaneously. I saw my blood flowing through my veins and arteries, my heart pumping rhythmically as my lungs emptied and filled; all the other organs, muscles, bones, were enveloped in clouds of energy, which directed, nourished and animated them. In some areas I spotted dark and dense blockages where the energy couldn't circulate properly. Inasmuch as the concentration of the energy was greater inside the blockages, the corresponding spots on the surface of my energy aura were gaping open like holes.

"The stranger moved his hand down my body and all the holes were filled and all the energy knots smoothed out. Now my aura resembled a flawless, shining egg. I raised my eyes to thank the stranger, but he was gone."

"Do you have any idea who he might be?" I asked.

"Not in the least," Tausha replied shortly.

I said thoughtfully, "I once heard from an old monk that a true vision is often followed by the presence of an Agent of Darkness. Do you think this might be what happened tonight?"

"I really don't know, though there was nothing at all sinister about the stranger. But the monk is right: the Dark agents do use the gap opened by an unusual influx of light."

"Can you still see through your body? Can you see through mine?"

"Wait a minute." Tausha focused his eyes and looked at me. "Yes, I can."

I must say I didn't feel at ease being X-rayed, so I went to the kitchen to make some tea. Tausha followed, took out his papers, and started to write. I noticed that his handwriting was inclined to the left. I read somewhere that this a sign of a gifted person.

Tausha ordinarily wrote for an hour or two every day. At that time he was completing a book on Kunta yoga as well as channeling an esoteric treatise, "The Sutra of the Crown," a highly symbolical collection of aphorisms about which he refused to comment before it was completed.

I put two cups of tea on the table, sat down, and watched Tausha. There was a saucer on the table with two lumps of sugar on it. Tausha was writing and drinking the tea, and I knew that in a few moments he would take one of the sugar lumps.

A queer idea suddenly came into my mind. I decided to *become* one of these lumps, that is, to enclose myself in one of the little white cubes, with two-to-one odds of being eaten by the Chief! Somehow I was certain that it mattered whether I chose the right one. Overcoming a moment of hesitation, I made up my mind, and no sooner had I become a sugar lump than Tausha took me between his fingers and ate me up.

10

*Right here and now, there is an invisible door. You have
passed right by it countless times. It is not hard to open,
just hard to see. Yet to find this door and open it is the
only reason you are here.*

After a few days, two of Tausha's companions joined us. They
were a study in contrast: scrawny Long John, whom I had already seen once, was dark and gloomy in appearance, while
Seryozha, a fragile young man from Sevastopol, radiated an everlasting smile.

Up until their arrival I had been alone with Tausha, and at first I
found their presence difficult to accept. Somehow a worm of posses-
siveness had crept into my heart. I knew that the apartment did not
belong to me anymore, nor, for that matter, did my life; but I was not
yet able to completely resign myself to this new path of non-attachment, though I was earnestly trying to do so. Tausha was conscious of
my predicament and gave me a brusque instruction: "Don't grasp
anything!"

I did not know then that it would take years of struggle to truly put
this principle into practice. It was also more difficult for me than for
John and Seryozha, who had already been trained as healers and were
away from Tausha for a few hours daily to work with their patients. I
had to catch up.

The core of Tausha's healing technique was opening yourself up to
the *source* of healing power and transmitting its "curative ray" through
one's hands and into the body of the patient. Tausha taught us that
different healing traditions delivered healing energy from different
sources. To get in touch with the specific source one had to be introduced to it—in other words, initiated.

The method of opening to the source and channeling the energy in
our tradition was an "emptying" meditation. All thoughts and emotions—even lofty ones—were considered to be nothing but hindrances.
Once initiated, you had to be perfectly still and empty: nothing to

worry or think about, nothing to do: just remain plugged in! The calmer you are, the stronger the channeled power.

Tausha warned us never to work out of pity, because pity leads one to try to heal the wrong people. "When you feel reluctant to work on a patient," he would say, "don't work on him. By no means can you heal all of the sick. Only heal *your* people. The flow will bring them to you."

Another principle was to trust yourself in general and your hands in particular. Hands have their own wisdom. If you let them go, they'll find the weak spots on the body intuitively. Doubt is a great obstacle at the beginning of one's practice, but eventually it goes away as one accumulates successes in the work.

Most diseases are caused either by a surplus of energy or a lack of it. The excessive energy in the organ or system makes the hand feel like it is absorbing it; deficient energy makes the hand emanate power. Usually the exchange of energy between organ and hand occurs simultaneously.

Tausha stressed the importance of protecting oneself against sickness that might be picked up from ones patients. Diseases tend to be transmitted energetically, for the bad karma behind the affliction must eventually be "burned off;" if the healer succeeds in preventing the sick person from having to burn it off him or herself, the healer will be in danger of taking it on, unless he or she is able to transform the negative vibrations.

A simple technique of protection is to put one's hands under a stream of cold water after a session; however, the principal means of protection is non-attachment. On the energy level this is channeling itself—healing without using your own resources. The philosophical principle of Karma yoga, non-attachment to the fruits of one's actions, displays here its practical application, for karma has no way of attaching to an unattached person!

In the course of practice, a healer learns how to use tactile sensations for diagnosis. Hot energy, for instance, definitely indicates an inflammation, whereas cancer gives a sensation like cold needles. Moreover, each disease has its specific subtle odor. Stomach ulcers smell like burnt rubber, kidney problems give out a marshy scent, etc. The most disgusting odor is the aroma of death—not the odor of a putrifaction, but one which appears some days before a person's demise. Even a healthy person gives out the death smell if destined to die. When I first opened up to this method of olfactory diagnosis, I had to stop using public transportation for a while, so heavily did public conveyances reek of the ailments of their passengers.

Tausha represented the inner energy structure of the body in terms of the traditional seven chakras, or energy centers, of yoga. Six of the chakras are responsible for physical disorders:

• The *Muladhara Chakra*, located at the base of the spinal cord, pertains to the diseases of the muscles and bones. This chakra produces the coarsest kind of prana—the earth element.

• The *Svadhistana Chakra*, located three fingers below the navel, relates to the diseases of the urino-genital system and the skin. Svadhistana works out the sexual energy or the water element.

• The *Manipura Chakra*, located at the solar plexus, corresponds to the diseases of all the organs below the diaphragm except the urino-genital ones. This chakra, which is the main vessel for storing energy in the body, produces the fire element, responsible for the digestion and the assimilation of food.

• The *Anahata Chakra*, located right in the center of the chest between the nipples, is associated with heart and lung problems. This center generates the energy for emotions. This kind of prana is associated with the air element.

• The *Vishuddha Chakra*, located at the base of the neck, is connected to ears, nose, and throat diseases. Vishuddha produces the element of ether, which lets us hear, smell and feel things.

• The *Ajna* or *Trikuta Chakra*, located between the eyebrows, relates to eye and brain dysfunction. This is the "third eye" center, responsible for clairvoyance. It produces Manas—the energy we use for thinking and seeing.

• The *Sarhasrara Chakra*, the seventh, located one finger above the crown of the head, in the aura, has nothing to do with physical problems. This is the center of intuition, the thousand-petaled lotus. The energy produced by this center is called *Odjas*.

These seven main chakras are usually depicted as flowers with various numbers of petals opening in the process of evolution. When in full bloom, all these energy flowers are open to the sun of the Absolute. This is the state of an enlightened individual, the crowning point of earthly evolution, traditionally represented by the symbol of a golden crown.

Despite having learned the theoretical part of energy healing, I could not imagine myself curing somebody with my hands. I struggled with my own scepticism for some time, and one day I approached Tausha, who was lounging in his armchair at the time, and confessed, "To tell you the truth, I doubt that I can heal anybody. I feel that something is missing."

"Come over here," Tausha demanded.

I came up to him. He told me to bend down, flicked me on the forehead, and said, "Go ahead."

For the first time I realized Tausha's magical power. Somehow I knew that now I would be able to heal. That was my initiation.

"What have you done?" I asked, amazed.

Tausha smiled in reply.

"Have you done something special or did you just 'flick' me?" I demanded.

Tausha kept smiling and said reassuringly, "Oh, I've definitely done something."

Only years later would I realize what he had done. He'd just flicked me on the forehead and said, "Go ahead."

11

Every situation that you have experienced, are now experiencing, or will ever experience was designed at the beginning of time by your true Self for your evolution. So there is no will that makes you and the world be the way they are other than that of your own Self at play. Behold!

A week went by. Long John and Seryozha had settled in. By that time I was extremely sensitive to the Dark Forces. I could easily feel their presence by the familiar cold thrill in my manipura chakra (solar plexus). It proved something I had often read about: at the beginning of the Path a neophyte is likely to encounter the demons and hungry ghosts of the lower regions of the "Astral" plane.

One evening, John and I were alone in the apartment. As we were sitting and idly chatting, the idea that we might try to invoke a hostile entity in order to test our ability to fight it off quixotically popped into my mind. After all, we considered ourselves to be warriors of Light!

We sat down cross-legged on the couch and assumed a serious expression. I began focusing on that hostile cold sensation. Suddenly we were in the midst of a veritable astral storm, and we lost all control over the situation.

On the floor, in the far corner of the room, there appeared a black jelly-like mass that started to grow rapidly and come toward us. We could see it with our physical eyes. It was as if horror, pain, and despair had taken material form and that we were staring at a heaving, gel-like, living brick or lump of matter, transported straight from Hell.

Terror-stricken, our limbs were literally frozen motionless, and we could do nothing but watch the ghastly show. The gel went on growing like a wad of infernal dough. It was quickly approaching the couch where we sat, and we thought we were about to be engulfed by it. But when it was a couple of yards away from us, it suddenly came to a halt and slowly emitted two long feelers with eye-like spheres on the ends of them. As soon as these spheres were formed, they began projecting hin energy rays directly at our hearts. It felt like we were being slowly executed by firing squad. The rays actually poked into the heart muscle and caused our heartbeat to become irregular.

We were already gasping for breath and seemed to be near our last gasp, when John started vocalizing in a desperate, deafening, high-pitched voice, the protective mantra "IM." I knew the mantra too, so I began chanting or rather yelling it simultaneously with him; apparently I was articulating the mantra properly enough, for the mantra saved us. In our desperation, we had cried out the mantra in the most precise way. A strange velvet ringing hung in the air. The deadly rays withdrew from our hearts, the feelers retracted, and the gel began shrinking and eventually melted away.

We got up and started moving around the apartment in the vain hope of regaining control of ourselves, but we could not stop shivering, and I was near panic. For the first time in my life I realized what it meant to be going mad. There is a certain fragile point of balance in the mind, and all the solid world around us exists only because that balance is maintained. Shift off this point a minute amount and an avalanche of madness is launched over your being; the world of reason collapses.

What matters here is the velocity of thought. We are accustomed to a certain thought ocurring at a certain speed, though we are ordinarily not aware of it. This thought speed is the frequency at which the "thought particles" are vibrating. If it changes, we begin slipping out of the rational frame of mind. Such was the case that evening. Thoughts were rushing through my head as if my mind tape had been switched from playback into rewind mode. Wherever they ran, they came to the edge of an abyss of madness. Every thought that came into my mind led to disaster. But I couldn't stop thinking!

I do not know what would have happened if we had been swept over that edge, but we were terrified of *possession*. We definitely felt that *some*body or some*thing* was present and ready to invade us and to take us over. I remember imaginging that if that happened, we would go on looking like ourselves, but inside we would become some kind of bio-robot, channeling alien orders. It would be worse than slavery. Something had to be done. Somehow we had to get control of the situation by regaining the power to focus our attention.

On the day of our little "experiment," I had been typing a copy of *The Gospel According to Thomas*. Under Soviet censorship, as I mentioned, copying banned books was a common way of distributing them. *The Gospel* was lying open on the table, and I suddenly ordered John to pick up the book and start dictating a passage to me. In a weak voice and stammering, John began dictating. I myself was so jittery I could hardly type. We had to summon all our strength just to perform this simple task. I don't remember what the words were, but in the end it seems the holy book did us a good turn. It was not all that long before we started giggling, and soon we burst into a nervous but hearty bout of laughter. Total relief.

All of a sudden Tausha blew in. It was 3 a.m. He had come by taxi, having picked up clarvoyantly what was going on.

"Idiots," he greeted us. "What the hell have you been up to?" We shrugged our shoulders. "We've been fighting demons," we told him sheepishly, and gave him an account, as best we could, of what had taken place.

"The road to Hell is paved with good intentions. All I need is two young corpses here!"

In spite of his annoyance, we felt at ease having the Chief at hand. What we had just been through no longer seemed quite real. I have since realized that encounters of this sort tend to appear imaginary shortly after they have happened. This distancing of the actual intensity of what we had been through allowed me to adopt something of a clinical perspective on it. I asked Tausha, "If we had died, what would be the medical explanation for our death?"

"Heart paralysis from fear," was Tausha's terse reply. "Touch wood."

"So that's how they kill you!"

"Directly, yes. But they've got other tricks too. They can drive you to suicide, for example."

"What do they do it for?" John asked.

"They feed on negative human emotions. There's an army of minor demons that love to gorge themselves on petty emotions like vexation or annoyance, but for such delicacies as horror or anguish the big guys come. Causing the Death of a human is not their motivation, however. They ordinarily prefer to possess a person alive, as they need living physical bodies for their activities.

"On the earthly plane all instances of warfare and tyranny are cases of temporary mass possession. When the possession of an individual becomes constant, the person either ends up in the mental hospital or becomes a conscious agent of the Rulers of Darkness. He may grow into a Stalin, a Hitler, or just turn out to be a serial killer.

"Some people get trapped fraudulently, lured by being offered power. This power, as a matter of fact, is actually delivered at first, but after you have played around with it for a while, you are compelled to pay with your most valuable treasure—your free will.

"To instigate all these complex interactions with human beings, the Dark Forces must maintain severe discipline. The KGB, as well as the Mafia and other criminal organizations, are successful because they resemble the Dark Hierarchy in structure, mimicking its discipline and enforcing it by the threat of imminent punishment in the case of failure. The material conditions for their activities are also identical: they live off human suffering."

"If demons feed on negative emotions," I asked, "who consumes the positive ones? The angels, dare I say? If so, the poor beings don't seem to be getting very fat off this earth."

"Cut your cynical attitude," Tausha snapped. "A mother seeing her kids happy doesn't feed on their joy, she shares it and gives it back a hundred times in return." He kept silent for a while, then added, "What is required of us now is a regimen of regular training. We'll begin tomorrow."

12

There are three Illusions. When a seeker enters upon the Path, first he searchs for a Teacher. In the process of the quest, or if he finds one, he realizes that the most important thing the Teacher can help with is the understanding that He is unnecessary. This is the awareness of the Illusion of the Teacher.

If the seeker moves on, he tends to believe that the place where he is at is not right for him. He should be somewhere else to find the Truth—another city, another country, another retreat, another room. So he moves around until he understands that it does not make any difference where he is. This is the awareness of the Illusion of Place.

When proceeding along the Path, there's always a hope, a hope for the future. It is presumed that the future holds something better in store for us. As the time passes by, the seeker realizes that nothing changes. Things are always the same. And this is the awareness of the last and greatest illusion—the Illusion of Time.

Upon awakening the next morning I had a strange experience of what I can only call "reversed time." With my eyes still closed, I was drawn back into the depths of dreamless sleep, and then I emerged into everyday consciousness again. In the few seconds or minutes that I was asleep, I was shown the structure of the subconscious mind. Unbelievably deep and fathomless it is! In the profound depths of the dreamless state lives our true "I," which is really not "I-like" at all. If I had to give it a name, I would call it "I-lessness."

What we consider to be ourselves is just a fragile snowflake on the tip of the iceberg of our subconscious. We resemble a cabbage or an onion with millennia of evolution and Karma imprinted on its layers.

In the process of awakening from deep sleep, we put on these layers the way we don clothes in winter. With each layer we become more and more structured, more and more programmed, more and more the familiar selves we know, until the last button is fastened and here we go, one billionth of what we really are, good morning!

After breakfast Tausha asked John and me to go out to buy some paints and Indian ink. I had not been outside for more than a week by this time, and it was quite an experience to see the city afresh. Tagging along with John, I felt quite ill at ease. I had become so sensitive that I found myself absolutely vulnerable to the city vibrations which seemed to be entirely alien and hostile to me now. I had to stay close to John to avoid being overwhelmed by insecurity. Later in my training I came to call this state the "dog effect." It happened to everyone who was assimilating Tausha's approach, and it generally took a few weeks before the neophyte achieved a new level of independence.

Seeing my embarrassment, John chuckled and slapped me on the back. "Hold on. I've been through the same difficulty. Come in under my cover." And he put his arm around my shoulder.

We resolved to take a shortcut to the store by metro. On the descending escalator I realized we had made a major blunder. The metro is very deep below the street in St. Petersburg, for the city had been set up on marshes. Furthermore, five of the central stations were built on the sites of demolished churches. There was definitely something *wrong* about the metro and I was feeling it in my guts. The further down we went, the worse I felt. In a panic and on the verge of fainting, I made a sudden lunge to climb up the descending escalator, but John was in my way. Once we reached the bottom, I leapt onto the ascending staircase and ran all the way up. Out in the open air, I felt better at once. We took a tram.

Returning home was an enormous relief. Tausha and Seryozha were there. Seeing my face, Tausha greeted us, "Welcome back to the bunker!" I lay down on the couch. John brewed up an herbal concoction and persuaded me to drink it. In half an hour I'd recuperated completely.

"All right, guys," Tausha said once I was functioning again, "I have an announcement. We've been *noticed*. The time has come to think about our own protection. We have to become much stronger in order to perform the kind of work we are about to do and survive it!"

"What about the protective Kunta symbols and mantras? They've worked pretty well so far," John said.

"They won't be enough from now on. We've been spotted by serious forces that don't want us to be doing what we are doing, and today we're starting a regular military training, as I promised yesterday. We've got to hold our ground."

"Why on earth should we fight at all?" I asked. After John's potion I felt quite relaxed and unwarlike. "The Dark and the Light forces originate from the same source, don't they? Why should we hold on to the view of that they are at war with each other, instead of breaking the illusion of their duality?"

Tausha explained patiently, "Because that is not our job. The plan is to establish the site of another reality in this gloomy world—a reality where the natural course of evolution can be restored. If you plant a tree, you have to fence it off until it's finished growing, otherwise it's going to be stepped on and destroyed. So for now we must protect our little energy garden as well as break fresh ground, since we've been given the blessing of 'the green beam' shining down on us right here."

"What's the source of the beam?" Seryozha broke in.

"What do you think?" asked Tausha, giving Seryozha a piercing look.

"My guess is Shambhala."

"You may be right, depending on what you mean by that," said Tausha. "The plan is to create a Shambhala-like place, a place hospitable to the flow, right here in the midst of the Soviet madness, in the city, not in a faraway retreat. We're not going to remain stuck in this apartment, however. When I say 'a place,' I don't mean a concrete location. I mean an energy structure, a sacred bowl filled up with energy and acting as an energy preserve.

"Traditionally, monasteries and shrines functioned as sacred containers of energy. But times have changed. Seclusion is not a necessity today. The ancient wisdom kept secret for ages is now being disseminated in the streets. A massive change in consciousness is under way.

"There is a unique opportunity for spiritual growth in Russia, for we combine an Eastern background with a Western outlook. Intuitive and rational approaches can be happily combined here. Decades of repression have not broken the spirit of the nation, and now it's entering a new stage of unfolding. It's up to us to make our contribution to the process and pave the way for the ones who will come later. So let's get down to business.

"I'd like you to study the basics of a martial art called Heiki. Heiki is an ancient art of energy wrestling as well as a self-defense technique. This is an easy thing to explain for it has only one rule: win without touching your partner." Tausha broke off as though assessing the level of our understanding.

We grew perplexed.

"So what are you supposed to do?" John asked.

"Follow Disa," said Tausha, flashing his unforgettable smile. "Do whatever you want, except don't touch your partner—but defeat him!"

Then Tausha stood up, told John to stand up, and ordered him to attack. John took a boxing stance and began moving around, looking for an opportunity to strike. Tausha was also moving, but in a different way. He was dancing around gracefully, keeping John at a distance. His movements did not in the least resemble the movements of combat. They were more like steps in a ballet.

Each time John approached Tausha, attempting to strike a blow, his hand seemed to get stuck in something and lost all its strength. Tausha, meanwhile, seemed to be enveloped in an invisible veil that absorbed the power of any aggressive move. There was something comical about the whole scene, as if Tausha were teasing John with his inaccessibility.

Growing exasperated, John dashed at Tausha unexpectedly with all the mass of his tall body. Tausha made a quick rejecting move and all of a sudden, as if being grasped by an unseen mighty hand, John was flung back and sent flying. He landed on the floor some yards away. In a moment he got up, safe but dumbfounded. The rest of us were too awestruck to utter a word.

That's how our "military training" began. To master Heiki skillfully would take a lifetime, but we started practicing on a regular basis, and we began to make progress within a few weeks. The technique benefited our energy development immensely, protecting us and increasing our sensitivity at the same time. Heiki turned out to be a meditation in motion.

The technique itself consisted of finding weak spots or gaps in the aura of one's partner and hitting them with energy impulses, while shielding oneself from the energy impulses coming from them. Tausha specified three initial Heiki styles: a Sword style, a Ball style, and an Empty style. Each style signified a different meditative approach, correlating to a specific psychic type.

Working in the Sword style you stretch the front side of your aura into the form of a blade or a spear. Being spearheaded against your partner, you probe for his gaps. You allow the incoming blows to slide along the blade sides. For the most part, however, this is an attacking style, requiring a lot of tension; it is the easiest of the three to perform.

In the Ball technique you form your aura into a ball and absorb the energy of your partner's blows. This makes you stronger and weakens your partner. Working in the Ball style, you do not protect yourself from the partner's attacks. On the contrary, you open yourself to them, since they become the source of your power.

The Empty style implies being emptied of the energy of aggression. You neither reject nor absorb it. You are transparent to the blows so they pass right through you and you remain unharmed. This is the most difficult style, for it has to do with non-attachment.

There are many more styles of Heiki—the Sun style, for example, in which you give your energy to your partner, transforming her attitude and making her unable to attack you. These additional styles were too advanced for us at this point, and Tausha never taught them to us. He mentioned, however, that the highest form of Heiki is non-action.

The accent in Heiki is on energy manipulation, not physical motion, although each style expresses itself through a special series of movements. These movements eventually become a spontaneous flow that looks much more like dancing, as they did in Tausha's original demonstration with John, than fighting. The appearance of of physical grace unmistakably indicates a high level of practice. Some postions of Heiki, however, are absolutely static, having to do solely with energy currents.

Besides producing an invigorating effect, a heightening of perception, and considerable progress in manipulating energy, experience with these Heiki styles brings insight into human relationships, since each style corresponds to a distinct behavioral pattern, as well as to a tactic of communication and a particular strategy for dealing with people.

13

Pondering on "how," you'll never manage. Just do it.

Tausha was reluctant to reveal his life story. The best I have been able to do is piece it together fragmentarily. For the most part his years before coming to St. Petersburg in 1979 are shrouded in mystery.

Tausha was born in a simple family in 1957 in Syktyvkar, the capital of the Komi republic in the north of Russia. His father was Komi, his mother Russian. In his school years Tausha was a rather reticent and withdrawn boy. He discovered his unusual abilities when he was fourteen.

Once, taking a walk along a river bank, he came across a drowned pigeon. The bird obviously had just been taken from the water by the children playing nearby, for it was still wet. Following a mysterious impulse, Tausha placed his hands over the pigeon and spent an hour trying to inspire life into its motionless body. He had begun to lose hope when the pigeon showed the first signs of animation and soon after flew away.

Tausha spent his vacation every summer with his grandparents in a remote northern village. Rural Russia has still preserved a lot of its medieval character. Every Russian village has its peculiar eccentric, its village "fool." The particular village where Tausha's grandparents lived was no exception. This fool was a widower and lived alone on a scanty pension. He kept himself apart from village life and never shared a word with others. It was rumored that he was mute. When the fool received his monthly pension, he would spend it right away in a small village shop. He would buy cheap canned goods, open the cans with his teeth, and devour the contents without leaving the shop. How he managed to support himself between pension payments was always a mystery.

His everyday occupation was utterly original. Every morning at dawn the fool would take an ax and go to the forest. There he would find a high fir tree, fell it, chop its top off and clean off the branches.

Then the villagers would see him coming home with this huge cudgel on his shoulder. The fool would accurately pile the branches up in his backyard, and, over the years, the pile turned into a mountain. Nobody could figure out why he would do such a thing. Apparently no one ever asked. People were afraid of him and preferred to keep away.

Once Tausha was on his way to going fishing and saw the fool sitting on the lake shore with a fishing rod. The boy was scared and halted, but the fool amicably waved him over. Tausha obeyed out of fear. When he approached the fool, Tausha saw him smiling, though none of the villagers had ever seen his smile before. He stroked Tausha's hair and began to speak with him in a friendly way. As the conversation developed, Tausha began to feel that this "fool" was really not only the wisest but the kindest person in the whole village. Later the two developed a relationship that resembled that of teacher and disciple. I do not know exactly what Tausha learned from the fool, but this encounter was probably the first step on his spiritual path.

The fool died the same weird way he had lived. He was crushed by a fir tree he was chopping. Apparently he had remained alive for a while after the tree fell, fighting to release himself, for the tree he was found under had been partly chopped away.

Town fools in general were far more than local peculiarities. From ancient times so-called "holy fools" or "God's fools" were well known all over Russia. People respected and feared them. Their madness was not an ordinary one, but was said to be a sign of divine grace. Their childish, often inappropriate behavior was believed to be the result of mental purity and spiritual advancement. Some of them could predict the future of the nation and, in a few cases, even influenced rulers, who both feared and respected them. The famous cathedral in Red Square in Moscow was named after the renowned Russian saint of the time, Vasily Blazhenny. The Russian word "blazhenny" is a synonym for "holy fool."

At the age of eighteen, Tausha was conscripted into the army. When he was asked to take his clothes off by the medical commission at the recruiting office, it was discovered that he was wearing a big cross beneath his shirt. The president of the commission, a colonel, demanded that he take the cross off. Tausha refused and was consigned for a month to a lunatic asylum. There he underwent psychotropic medication for the first time. Before the end of his term, Tausha managed to escape. Soon after that he went to St. Petersburg and became a student in the biology department of the university. Thus he avoided army service.

He was only a student for a year however, for he was expelled because of his interest in the occult and in religion generally. At that time not only was *publishing* mystical literature illegal, but even *reading* it was as well.

After his expulsion he started wandering across the Soviet Union searching for people who could be helpful in his spiritual quest. During his travels he met a few remarkable characters. One of them was a Ural village healer who could heal practically any disease. His method was simple and effective. The patient was asked to supply a bottle of vodka, while the healer provided a snack. After a friendly chat and mutually finishing off the bottle, the patient would simply depart from the healer, completely healed of whatever happened to have been his complaint. It didn't matter whether it was a cancer or a cold. All his cases were equally successful. Tausha made friends with him and stayed at his place for some time. When he spoke of him he would always refer to him as "an ideal Russian healer."

Tausha discovered through this healer's son the circumstances surrounding his death. The son was working at a construction site somewhere in Siberia, thousands of miles from his father's village. One day he went upstairs to the garret of the barracks he lived in. It was a dark, dusty room full of junk. Suddenly he saw his father. Astonished, the healer's son asked him what he was doing there. His father said that he had died and had come to bid him farewell. The next morning a telegram arrived, informing the son of the healer's death.

Another remarkable acquaintance of Tausha was an old disciple of Gurdjieff named Malhas Gargiani. Georgi Gurdjieff, the famous spiritual master whose philosophy and teaching originated from the Sufi tradition, had an extensive following internationally, which is still active today. The "Work," as he called it, carried out the special mission imposed on him by a secret Sufi Order. Gargiani was a highly intelligent and well-educated person, a physician and an astrologer who lived in Tbilisi, the capital of Georgia. One of his gifts was an ability to project an intended image onto a blank plate using only his bare hands.

Apparently, Gargiani made a considerable contribution to Tausha's spiritual evolution. Among other things, he introduced Tausha to a unique Georgian way of healing insanity by singing. He took him to a distant mountain village where a few old people were still capable of performing this ancient practice, and Tausha had a chance to witness it first hand.

As Tausha described this event, at dawn a group of old villagers gathered at a gorge and made a cirle holding each other's hands, placing the sick person in the center of it. After a prayer, they began to chant a sacred, seven-voiced canon. The sound of the ancient chanting was echoed and amplified by the walls of the ravine, reverberating in the most incredible way.

The patient was affected almost immediately. He began to shiver, convulsively screaming out in a bizarre voice that was not his own. Then he fell down and started to roll around, trying to break out of the circle. His eyes rolled, and foam appeared on his lips. In spite of the ugly scene, the singers kept on chanting firmly and melodiously, not letting the patient escape from the circle. After a while he calmed down and sank into a sort of trance followed by a long deep sleep that resulted in a complete recovery.

At Gargiani's, Tausha had his first experience of seeing auras. Malhas taught him Gurdieff's exercise of seeing things with each eye independently. This exercise is intended to expand the range of one's vision beyond the world of solid matter. The exercise is simple: stand before a half-open door, its butt-end between your eyes so that you see both the inside and the outside of the room, keeping both spaces in focus simultaneously.

After practicing for some days, Tausha went up to a window and looked out. It was a sunny weekend and the street was filled with people. Over the crowd, Tausha was able to see a radiating, ever-changing rainbow composed of the people's auras. This shining rainbow displayed every possible tint and color, interflowing and interchanging constantly. The sight was just magnificent. Emanated by each individual, the rainbow nevertheless appeared to be one beautiful, living, and immortal being.

Once I asked Tausha how he first came across Disa. He said that Disa had come to him in the Pamir highlands when he was trekking along a narrow mountain trail. The trail meandered along the edge of a precipice, squeezed by a vertical rock wall. All of a sudden, Tausha was confronted by a herd of sheep on the run, headed by a full-grown male with huge crooked horns. The trail was too narrow to pass, and there was no place to hide between the rock wall and the abyss. Tausha had only a couple of seconds to find his way out. He did what his body told him to do. He stopped dead, threw his hands up impetuously and roared. The lead sheep leapt off the trail and disappeared into the chasm. The others, including the lambs, followed. Tausha lost sight of them. He approached the site of the jump and leaned over the brink. To his amazement, he saw the herd safe and sound, climbing the rocks far below. Obviously, the sheep's skill in mountain trekking was far beyond human comprehension.

Thinking this incident over, Tausha came to the conclusion that his life had been saved by following without hestitation an intuitive impulse—the practice he would eventually call Disa. To fling out his hands and to roar was precisely what it occurred to him that he could do in that seemingly hopeless situation. Working the Disa principle out later, he discovered that there is one thing a person is actually always certain of—what he or she wants.

The intuitive wish impulse is forever alive. This is a pure manifestation of the ever-flowing life force, accessible anywhere, anytime. Each intuitive wish impulse has its secret wisdom. Never senseless, it always implies a means to reach the goal through opening to the eternal source of all the wishes—to Almighty God, returning to Himself along the thorny path of earthly life.

Practicing Disa does not mean satisfying absurd fantasies which, in fact, are not wishes at all but just fantasies. Real wishes are simple and actual. Performed sincerely, free from fear and egotism, they inevitably lead to self-knowledge and ultimately to the revelation of the mysteries of the universe.

It was in the Pamir mountains that Tausha met the man who would become his Master. Tausha did not tell much about his years of discipleship, and at no time did he mention where it had taken place. He spent some years in Pamir at a secret center of ancient knowledge belonging to the Shambhala tradition. Hidden deep in the wilderness of the highlands and practically inaccessible, the center was impossible to reach without being invited and guided.

Tausha first met his teacher in a little Tadjik mountain village in a tea-house, where he called Tausha by his name and ordered him brusquely, *"Follow me."* They walked for eleven days, sleeping in caves that seemed to have been intentionally placed along their route.

Tausha never spoke of how he had been trained at the center. The only thing he mentioned was that his Disa practice had been completed there. He was taught that this technique was a true one, but fell short of helping one realize the totality of perception. To trace one's wishes back to their source and to eliminate the difference between wants and actions, that is, to become sincere in one's pursuits, is only half of the process. The other side of the coin is to accept the world as it is, without differentiating it into the desirable and the unwanted, the painful and the pleasurable. By fighting a reality that we are not able to accept, we are fighting God's will instead of cooperating with it and letting it work through us. Through this fighting, not only do we lose a great deal of our energy, but we block ourselves from an unspeakably mightier power which is always ready to come.

When a bowl is full, it overflows naturally. A genuine, spontaneous action is nothing other than this overflow, driven by abundance, not by scarcity.

In order to give, one should learn to accept. One needs to surrender and accept in order to become full, but this does not mean being passive. True acceptance is not a one time act; it is a process, a flow of the inseparable totality of perception. To act out of this fullness means being generous in a natural way. Most of us act out of necessity or need. The sense that we are fundamentally lacking distorts the truth that every individual is a child of God, capable of tapping into the source of Divine abundance. Only through abundance can we really share.

Tausha arrived in St. Petersburg, which was still Leningrad, in 1979. There he got in touch with John and Seryozha, his ex-fellow university students, and they became his first followers. Tausha was now performing healing for a living, and through this field he became acquainted with Nana, who was a rather intriguing personality. She was a bundle of intense, humorous and mischievous energy.

Nana was a Gypsy and had been a fortune-teller. Over time she had developed the gift of clairvoyance. Nana worked for the police for a while, helping to locate missing people, and became so good at it that she ended up being spotted by the KGB. Nana was offered "an interesting job" in the psychic research field with a high salary. The job involved participation in secret programs such as the development of psychic weapons, as well as working as a human lie detector to see if what an accused person said was true.

Nana felt trapped, for once you were working for the KGB, there was no turning back. Though she falsely declared a loss of her psychic powers, she was not left in peace. She had a family, and the KGB did not miss this opportunity to blackmail and intimidate her. When Nana met Tausha through one of his patients, she was on the verge of committing suicide.

Tausha was aware that there were quite a number of extremely talented psychics working in the KGB secret laboratories that were reportedly filled with millions of dollars worth of research equipment. An idea of undermining the KGB by converting some of those people to the Path of Light was ripening in his mind, and meeting with Nana gave it a chance. When I showed up, this project had already been set into motion.

14

Be who you are. There is a mystery inside you, and to discover it is the most difficult thing on earth. In attempting to become somebody else, you lose the chance. To unveil the mystery, you should stop trying on various ous masks and see your soul as it is—pervading everything.

One evening during our second week together, Tausha was teaching Seryozha and John to play "Skip." Skip is a sophisticated board game that we surmised Tausha had brought from the Pamir center. When we asked him about its origin, he was evasive and turned it into a joke.

The game vaguely resembled chess with the difference that the board was blank, and every figure, made of a jade-like stone, had a specific energy potential. The realization of that potential varied depending on the stone's position on the board. The harmonious arrangement of one's figures enhanced their ability to trap or to repel one's opponent's figures. Once overcome by an attacking figure's energy field, the opponent's stones could be dismissed from the board. The game was an excellent way of training the intuition and heightening one's level of perception.

I was sitting by, watching the game, when something made me look up. In an upper corner of the room, under the ceiling, I caught sight of a small being hanging in the air. My first reaction was merely surprise, but in an instant I knew who it was. I stood up and uttered in a faltering voice, "The Prince."

Tausha gave me a look of instantaneous understanding. Somehow I realized that only he and I knew who had come. In an instant something soft but forceful penetrated my solar plexus and my whole body went limp; I fell down, almost in slow motion. Now I was prostrate on the floor, completely disoriented, and oddly unable to relate to what was going on around me.

My friends' faces were all blurry and at the same time seemed far away. I didn't feel any pain, just an overwhelming sense of indifference.

Everything seemed to have lost its significance. I was taken to the bedroom and put on a couch. I lay there quietly and without complaining, so they shut the door and left me alone.

It was my first encounter with the Prince of the World, and what struck me most about Him was the great difference between Him and the demons, like the one I had already encountered. His subordinates are all gross characters—butchers, really, as Tausha had explained. All they have on their minds is to possess their victims—to suck the life force out of them and ultimately to kill them with terror. To attain these goals, the demons apply two principal tactics—a ray blow and what amounts to a kind of physical pressure. The ray blow is a means of assault. The pressure is more like an energy blockade.

But the Prince has nothing to do with butchery. He is a cosmic spirit of the highest rank and of an indescribable power. His vibrations are impossible to mistake. Being of an extremely subtle and sublime nature, they *almost* inspire reverence. In fact, to the unwary, they *do* inspire reverence! He is a lord and a ruler here, there is no question about it.

I learned later that it is impossible to summon the Prince. He comes of His own accord and only for a serious purpose. There is something very personal about His touch. He might appear to you in a crowd, but you would be the only one to see him, and you would be as alone with Him there as you might be in a desert. If He comes, He comes just for you, blocking you off from everything, even, or particularly, from God. It is almost impossible to pray in His presence. Those who have not encountered Him in some sense previously, are unable to recognize Him.

After a while, slumped there on the couch, I began to feel very bad. I could not move. I tried to call for Tausha's help, but I had lost my voice and the shut door blocked my rasping whisper. I thought I was dying. At last the door opened and Tausha came in. He sat down silently by my side and started massaging my solar plexus. In half an hour I was able to get up.

"Congratulations," Tausha said, once I had been more or less restored to my normal state. "You've been introduced at Court."

"Should I esteem it an honor?" I said sarcastically. "Why did He come? Why did he *hit* me?"

"Ten or fifteen minutes before his arrival, you mentioned His name disrespectfully! He was giving you a lesson. He struck a blow in your

Manipura chakra. From now on—mind your speech."

From then on there was a new fear in my heart, afear of quite a different quality from the cold and eerie feeling that lodged in me when I used to bring the the long-eared creature or the jelly-like substance to mind. With the latter, I was afraid for my mental and physical health, but the Prince was a threat to my soul, the loss of which was more terrifying to me than anything in the world.

Eventually my helplessness before Him became unbearable, and within a month of the encounter I resolved to do something about it. It seemed that the only way to extinguish my fear was to pray for Him, but I was not positive that such a prayer was possible. In his presence, the very *meaning* of prayer seemed unavailable to the mind or heart. Yet to pray for him without his being present wouldn't dispell my fear. I asked Tausha if praying for Satan was allowed or even possible. Tausha quipped: "Do it if you've really set your heart on it, but keep your heart firm and your fingers crossed!"

Since I knew that I had to offer up my prayer in Lucifer's presence, and since I also knew that he couldn't be summoned, I had to wait for a time when He Himself chose to make His next visit.

The Prince's next visit was paid in an overcrowded winter bus where I was sandwiched in between a policeman and a fat lady in a fur coat. When the Prince appeared, everything else faded away. I was alone with him. I can only say that for all its horror—which was immense— his presence was what I can only call elevating, profound, and absolutely breathtaking. I was filled with awe.

He had came to offer me power. He said He had sent his butchers to test my spirit and I had passed the test. He said that *His* evolutionary Path was different from the Path of the Light Forces—more hazardous, so to speak. But if He won, the spiral of His and His team's evolution would skyrocket. He said that His advantages were speed and discipline. Everything was quick in His world, and if I agreed to work with Him, I would be given an immense power and new opportunities right away.

This was his message. The Prince was waiting for my answer. Here was my chance. My task was to stay crystal clear and keep my heart open. I felt that the slightest hesitation—either in the way of being tempted by his offer or being overwhelmed by loathing for what he was—would ruin me. I summoned all my courage and stepped into the breach. I visualized Christ standing behind the Prince and, penetrating his presence with my invocation, I sent a prayer for Satan to Jesus with all my might. The prayer was heard. I experienced a tremendous rush of relief sweep through me. Both Lucifer and my fear of Lucifer were gone. I stepped off the bus a different person.

When I described this event to Tausha, he gave me a hug and commented, "Fear is our own energy, working against us. It chases us like a predator chases its prey. You were able to turn the situation around, reversing the current of energy. The nature of fear is aggression; it can't stand to be chased. When you stopped fleeing and faced your fear with your heart open, you became the predator; the fear became the prey and ran away.

"In this empire of evil called the USSR, fear-related problems are everywhere. You are perceiving their causes on the subtle plane now. That's why you've been through all these encounters lately. It will change soon. When you lose your interest in the Dark Forces and stop being scared of them, they will lose their grip on you.

"Don't relax, though. The Prince is not the last issue. He is just one black hole among many. The center of evil is real, and it has many ways of manifesting, not only in the form of he Prince. Underestimating its might can be a mighty blunder."

I must have made a sour face for he added, "Take it easy. You are on the point of rising to a higher plane. Just don't hurry. Take your time. By the way, it's high time that you begin your healing practice. You could probably help people with fear-related health concerns. I'm going to provide you with your first patient."

This first patient turned out to be a man suffering from a nervous breakdown that occurred under rather unusual circumstances. Here is his story.

Trains are the most popular means of transportation in Russia. One day a train pulled into a station, and, after boarding, three well-dressed men approached the conductor of the sleeping car. Two of them were quite sober and seemed respectable, but the third appeared to be dead drunk, and his two friends were forced to carry him on their shoulders. Their tickets were all in order, but the conductor refused to let the drunken passenger on—as the others might have expected—until she was bribed. When negotiations were completed, she showed them to their compartment and ceremoniously commanded them to behave. The compartment was designed for four passengers, so one seat remained unoccupied.

At the next station, a new passenger entered the compartment, so now it was full. This new passenger in fact was a professional thief. Seeing one of the men totally drunk and unconscious, he decided to wait until his companions went to the dining car and then check his pockets.

When the men finally went out, the thief hit the sleeping drunkard on the head with a bottle just to be on the safe side. But he was in for a surprise. The blow had been too strong and the thief realized that instead of stunning the person, he had killed him. The others were due to be back in a few minutes, so what could he do to avoid being caught red-handed?

The thief began to panic. He opened the window and with great exertion managed to heave the corpse out of it. Just as he finished, the men returned. They looked around and asked where their "drunk friend" could be. The thief answered that he had just left for the restroom and would certainly be right back. The two men turned white as a ghost.

In order to save money on the transportation of the body of a deceased relative, the men had fitted the corpse out with traveling clothes and were doing their best to pretend that they were accompanying a drunken friend. It was one of those two men that was to be my first patient!

15

Be still.

As time passed, Tausha put us through the mill with a variety of rigorous training methods. Along with traditional approaches such as meditation, chanting, visualization, energy healing, and calligraphy, he introduced us to many practices that I had never heard of before. Some of them were game-like, such as "Hap," the name of which obviously originated from the English word "happening." Others were more complex and profound.

Hap is a game that has no rules. Two players (though there can be more) are given a minute during which they can do whatever they want or nothing at all. The aim is simply "to win." A third person acts as referee. The person who behaves in the most spontaneous and natural way gains a victory. It's a mental-energy combat between the states of mind of the two players. In spite of its seeming simplicity, Hap is not so easy.

Even more difficult to master was the reading of the "Akashic records." The Akasha is a layer of ether that envelops the Earth, a kind of spiritual recording tape on which all the information of the past is recorded. Tausha shared the view of the ancient teachings that all the events that have ever taken place on Earth or in the cosmos remain imprinted on the ether, and in the same way present events are being imprinted there at the present moment.

Through special visualizing and breathing techniques, he taught us how to tune in to the most subtle vibrations of the ether that carry the stored information from the past. It is a mine of knowledge. Any information can be obtained, as long as it has not been intentionally sealed; the data pertaining to one's own karmic history, for instance, is easily accessible.

Eventually Seryozha scored a great success with this technique. He could describe in precise detail the remote events of the past, giving the exact timing and the names of the participants of the events, which we would check later in history books or in an encyclopedia; he could also describe what had happened to a person yesterday. He was unable to say anything about the future, however. Tausha explained that the accurate reading of the future is quite a different thing, requiring much more energy and effort.

The next step after learning to read the Akashic record was to develop an ability to learn chosen disciplines from astral instructors. Tausha revealed to us that no lore is hidden from a student craving knowledge. All the wisdom acquired by people from all the ages is always accessible not just by delving into dusty books but through live, vibrating contact with the guru. The Masters of the past have not gone away. Living in different dimensions, they are forever ready to respond to a genuine seeker.

The main point is to determine precisely the subject you really want to study. Astral learning is a matter of one's own free will. The teachers in subtle bodies, unlike Zen masters, do not have a stick to hit you with. So the main thing that induces one's progress is self-discipline. That does not come easily. The process of learning tends to be elusive in the beginning.

I chose to study a basic set of exercises that had been taught at the ancient Egyptian schools for priests. Tausha helped me to get in touch with the soul of an Egyptian priest who had attained liberation in his lifetime in Egypt and had never reincarnated since. The priest told me his name and forbade me from revealing it to anyone. In this case, as in many esoteric traditions, the name plays the role of a sacred key, providing access to information possessed by its bearer.

To master the exercises, I was given four information "channels."

The first channel was an energy impulse received by my body so that I could feel the correctness or incorrectness of a movement with my flesh and bones. Say I start moving my hand. This had to be done in a slow and relaxed manner. The impulse unmistakably guided me as to where and how I should terminate the movement in order to be in the right position and in what direction I should continue next. The impulses came intermittently at first, but once I had mastered following them, they flowed together. My body was taught to move, directed by an uninterrupted energy flow which ceased if I made a wrong move. This continuous flow of energy was the second channel.

The third channel was a verbal one. In case I did not understand something, I could put a question telepathically and get an answer right away. If I still could not grasp it, I was shown a picture. Usually I saw a tall man with a shaved head in a white robe. He stood in a sandy courtyard with beautiful carvings on the walls and performed the exercise I was having difficulty with. Access to this instructor was the fourth, or visual channel.

The amount of information attainable through these four channels was more than enough for making steady progress in the exercises. However, the worm of doubt was still alive in my heart, so one day I asked Tausha, "How can I be sure that I'm not fantasing all this information?"

Tausha answered, "Don't impoverish the Universe with your mental limitations. Whatever you are able to imagine, and infinitely more than that, exists somewhere as a reality. As a matter of fact, it is an illusion that we can imagine anything. The mind works more as a receiver than as an inventor. Properly trained, it is able to perceive unimaginable realities that are beyond any rational grasp. What you call your fantasy, your imagination, is really a receiving instrument, but for this very reason, even the slightest doubt blocks reception, because it causes the imaginative process to stop in its tracks. Remember Christ's drowning disciple on the Sea of Galilee? On the other hand, it does make sense to check one's contacts with astral beings to make sure that you are not completely off the wall. This is easy to do, and is different from ordinary doubting. Don't interrupt any contact while it is happening, but check the consequences of the instructions imparted in your everyday life. Real contact with Beings of Light dramatically changes your way of life in a positive way. If your life continues to run on the same old track inspite of what you are learning, no matter how euphoric or interesting the experience might be, you are trapped by the force of illusion.

"In case you need a quick check, listen to your heart. From the moment it starts talking to you, it can never tell a lie."

While I appreciated the uniqueness of Tausha's enterprise, at the same time, given the conditions of Soviet totalitarism, I felt its fragility. Once Tausha had refused to take part in the official parapsychology research projects, our group was not safe. Tausha had been spotted by the KGB even before he met Nana as a result of a successful healing session: the spouse of one of his patients turned out to be a KGB officer. Tausha was also attempting to infiltrate the projects themselves. Through Nana, who had joined the group a little earlier than I, Tausha had contacted a few prominent psychics who were participating in certain secret KGB-supported studies. He did not talk much about these contacts, however.

I still was harboring dreams of devloping my practices in a remote natural setting, and one day, while talking to Nana, I suggested to her that perhaps we might move our work somewhere else for a couple of years, perhaps to a Siberian village. Everything I knew about Tausha's hazardous relations with the KGB I had found out through Nana. She shared my anxiety about the danger Tausha and the work was in and was delighted with the idea. We decided to discuss it with Tausha.

One day when all five of us were present at the apartment, I asked Tausha what he thought of moving to a remote part of the country in order to accomplish our training in a safer environment.

"No," was his reply. "There's no such thing as 'accomplishing' the training. I'm learning the same way you are. Instead of running away, we are going to do the opposite. We are going to expand our activities. We'll start an expansion soon."

He stayed silent for a while, then winked at Nana. "By the way, what's up at the KGB?"

Nana broke into laughter. "As usual, good news. A new subdepartment of the bureau that deals with psychics, mystics, paranormal phenomena and religion has been set up to be in charge of the KGB's dealings with the Hare Krishna movement, which has now been around for quite a while. Well, the lieutenant-colonel, a man in his forties, who was assigned to head the new subdepartment, dropped dead from a heart attack the day after he received his new assignment. According to the Hare Krishna teachings, chanting the name of Krishna is the basic means of salvation—and the Hare Krishna people say: 'Lucky is the person who has the name of Krishna on his lips before he passes away.'

"Anyhow, they let it be known that this is what would happen to anybody appointed to this post. The officers of the department tend to be very superstitious because of their work, so the position is vacant to date."

When our uproarious laughter faded away, Nana went on seriously, "There is sad news, too. Secret statistical research has been conducted lately, indicating incontestably that the number of children born with innate ESP abilities has increased dramatically within recent years and is continuing to grow. I managed to look through some reports on the subject. There are cases of children, mostly in rural communities in remote areas, born with ability in telepathy, clairvoyance, clairaudience, telekinesis, and even levitation.

"There is no scientific explanation for this phenomenon so far. There are just some working hypotheses supposing that it might be a kind of mutation stimulated either by dispersed radiation or cosmic rays. Most of the parents of these kids, ignorant of the nature of the phenomenon, consult with doctors. After that, the children are usually put into psychiatric hospitals where they are successfully ruined by strong medications instead of being given special care!

"The worst part of it is that the KGB is well aware of the value of these kids and is showing a definite interest in them. I've got information that they are planning to set up a boarding school of a closed type with special development programs aimed at evolving paranormal abilities. I think, if it's launched, this project might have a terrible outcome."

Tausha nodded. "No question about that. A parade of psychics in uniforms would be a spectacular scene. Russia is not the only country where a splash of ESP abilities among kids has been noticed. Another place is Brazil.

"I've been thinking of starting a spiritual school for kids myself. I see it as a center where different spiritual approaches might be synthesized. At schools now, children are taught anything but genuine spirituality, so what can we expect for the future if we don't give kids the basics? As for actually inaugurating such a school, however, given present conditions, it's too soon even to speak about it."

Tausha cast a glance at us and added, "By the way, there's one thing you are right about: we must move out of here."

"When? And where to?" asked John.

"To some other apartment. Within two hours."

16

Karma reveals itself in the endless current of thoughts and images rushing through the mind. To be able to direct this current is to be in command of your existence.

You are the creator: You create reality by the power of your thought, attracting into your life whatever you think of. Your present world is the result of your past thoughts. As for your future, ask yourself, "What kind of a future am I thinking up for myself right now?"

We did not argue, though it seemed pretty silly to give up an apartment we felt so comfortable in. But it was our Master's Disa and we obeyed without dissent because we *wanted* to do so. Tausha never forced us to do anything. Discipline came easy to us since our trust in him had become unconditional.

Ever-resourceful Nana called her girlfriend Nelli and reported to us that Nelli was willing to let us stay at her place for a while. Everyone gathered their things and off we went.

Nelli made her living as a cook and lived with her five-year-old daughter in a two bedroom apartment that was as bare as a convent cell and was located in the heart of the old city. This district is traditionally called "Dostoevsky's Petersburg," as most of the events described in Dostoevsky's novels take place within it. The area is of a distinct historical character but, as readers of Dostoevsky know, dark and gloomy in appearance.

Nelli's apartment was on the ground floor and faced a typical old Petersburg yard—a square piece of asphalt without a patch of greenery, surrounded by yellow. Petersburgers call those yards "wells."

I had met Nelli a few times before and what I liked about her was her strong character. She was deeply unsatisfied with the tedious routine of a single mother's life and retained the unbroken spirit of a true "seeker." Nelli welcomed us warmly and soon joined our team without hesitation or doubt.

As Nelli began to work with us, I was able to observe that a female's reaction to the energy flow differs from a male's. A woman lets the flow in as soon as she gets the feel of it. Instead of asking questions, she just gives in, opening her heart right away. She senses the enlivening power with every fiber of her body and needs no argument to surrender. On the other hand, a woman is less persistent in the truth-seeking pursuit and more easily falls a prey to distraction. She gets more interested in the very process of experiencing the flow, which she enjoys a lot, than in advancing towards the goal by means of it.

It is harder to get a man involved—he has to be either persuaded or trapped. The flow can initially repel a man, as he smells a threat to his ego. But once on the path, he is more centered, and his commitment to reach freedom is more likely to grow unshakable.

Two days after we moved to Nelli's, my friend Felix (to whom I had left my apartment and who had not joined our group, despite all my efforts to get him interested) informed me that the the apartment had been sealed up by the police. To avoid the risk of talking on the phone (for any phone line in the country might be bugged), we met in person, and he told me what had happened.

Soon after our departure Felix and two fellow-students arrived at the apartment in high spirits. While they were drinking and chatting, one of them, an Armenian, went to the bathroom and stayed there long enough to make his friends worry. He did not answer their calls, and after forty minutes or so, when the two were about to break the door, the Armenian leapt out of the bathroom. He was shaking all over and a weird expression was playing over his face. The poor man looked completely demented. The metamorphosis was a drastic one, for everybody had known the Armenian as a good-natured, well-balanced person.

Screaming out ominous threats and obscene curses, the crazed fellow grabbed a heavy leaden baby's tub that stood on the bathroom floor and threw it at Felix. Felix just managed to dodge the potentially mortal impact, pulled off his military waist belt and hit the Armenian on the head with its massive buckle. Shocked by the blow, his face bleeding, the Armenian stormed out of the apartment, and that was the last that was ever seen of him.

Unnerved by the incident, Felix and his companion left shortly afterwards, not being aware of the fact that the neighbors had called the police because of the noise. The police came, broke the door down, searched the apartment and sealed it up. Spotting the police car at the doorway the next day, Felix realized that the apartment had been closed.

"Those damn yogis have screwed up such a nice place!" he thought to himself, but since the apartment did not belong to him, there was no way for him to reclaim it from the police.

When I told Tausha what had happened, he commented, "It was the assault we've managed to escape."

I did not understand. "What happened to the poor Armenian? Why was he afflicted?"

"The Armenian became a target after we disappeared. Remember I told you that we had been spotted by some serious forces?

I nodded.

"I hope you didn't think I meant the KGB! Well, when we left your apartment and settled down here at Nelli's, I removed the protective energy shield and established it over here. The energy channel we had built there, however, stayed open for some time afterwards and subsequently was used by our opponents."

"Can the Dark Forces use the same channels as the Forces of Light?"

"Yes, they can. The energy is neutral in itself. Everything depends on its application."

"But why the Armenian, not us? The guy was innocent!"

Tausha grinned, "There's no such thing as 'innocent.' The very fact of having a body points to our imperfection. Besides, never forget that we may yet pay the price ourselves. If we hadn't left when we did, I just don't know what would have happened. The structure of the energy mesh we built there was connected to the place itself."

"Will the new tenant go mad at Nelli's when we move out?"

"No. Now we are capable of creating the mesh in a form that is unattached to place. We are able to hold the beam by our group energy, without having to ground it in our location."

As the group mastered a set of practices, Tausha added more. One of the new exercises was called "shadow." It was a training in invisibility. The task was to become imperceptible to other people.

On the meditation level it meant identifying oneself with nothingness, absolute void. One had to reverse the habitual pattern of considering oneself "something" by thinking of oneself as "nothing." A customary state of being "full" was to be dissolved into the state of being as empty as "an old cracked pot."

On the practical level "shadow" turned out to be a weird practice. First Tausha sent each of us in turn to crash parties at the homes of people we did not know. As soon as we succeeded in not being thrown out, we became eligible for the next step. The series was nothing but the art of deception. For instance, one had to slip into a movie theater without a ticket or slip onto a bus right under the ticket-collector's nose. Some of our attempts landed us in police stations.

Another exercise was in "inaudible talk." An experienced mantra chanter knows that sometimes a mantra passes out of the earshot of those who are not in tune with the chanter. Using a special attuning technique, Tausha taught us how to modulate our voices in chanting so that they could be heard only by the participants.

Later came words. Beginning with whispering, we eventually learned how to talk louder and louder, until we were able to yell at one another in the street, unheard by the surrounding crowd!

In the evenings, we held group meditations. They were guided by Tausha when he wanted us to carry out some particular task, but most of the time we just sat silently with the Master, letting the flow change us.

Tausha used to say that there must be no difference between meditation and daily life and that we meditate the way we live and we live the way we meditate. He therefore refrained from dictating how we should meditate and gave us freedom of choice in conducting the practices he disclosed.

When Tausha did guide our meditations, I would occasionally see a tall, effulgent, cloud-like figure hovering behind him. When I mentioned this to him, he explained that the figure was his teacher, who had begun to manifest visibly to Tausha after his experience of Christ's incursion.

One evening, after an extremely elevating group meditation, I asked Tausha what he thought of how we were getting on. The Chief was in the process of leaving at that moment. Holding the door half-open, Tausha turned back and said calmly, "Everything went fine, only God was forgotten." Then he walked out, shutting the door an inch away from my nose.

17

Find the sun by its rays.

Living beneath an incessant downpour of energy turned out to be a totally new experience for each of us. The precious flow bestowed on the group in response to our commitment and wholehearted practice was growing in intensity and scope day in and day out. The constant stream of ever fresh life force, which we invariably appreciated as Grace, fused life and practice into an indivisible whole.

What is life in the flow like?

The flow starts with the transformation of the physical body. Just as withered leaves regain their lushness and luster in the monsoon rain, so the body cells open and become vibrant and cheerful in the animating torrent. The whole organism wakes up and reaches toward the vital source of its vitality, which almost becomes more important to it than food or drink. The need for material sustenance and sleep is in fact enormously reduced in the presence of what is the ultimate essence of nourishment and rest. All fatigued or unhealthy organs and systems of the body receive the best cleansing and healing possible, to which the body responds with an overwhelming feeling of *gratitude*. And along with its new-found vitality, it takes on a new (or, maybe just long forgotten) function of perceiving, absorbing and accumulating the blissful invisible light.

The flow's impact is not limited to bodily or even psychic transformation. The current demands all of you, and if you take the plunge with your whole being, it turns your mind and body into a precious channel for primordial, pristine awareness, which overflows through you into the world with the purpose of perfecting both you and your world.

The emanation of the flow through and from your presence is easily sensed by all creatures. I observed that cats and flowers are particularly sensitive to it. Cats always come and sit by the healer's side during a healing session. They purr and rub against him or her in appreciation of the energy. Cut flowers, irradiated by the palm of the healer's hand once a day, may stay fresh for weeks.

The practical applications of the bodily emanation are innumerable. For instance, given the often unsanitary quality of Soviet food, we used it to disinfect our meals. Once I gave a bottle of "charged" water to an old woman. She found it so beneficial for her health that she came over for a new bottle every other week from then on. She mistook the water for church holy water and I did not try to dissuade her from thinking so. John joked that I might do well opening an energy-charged soft-drink business!

The flow allows one to greatly increase one's capacity for Hatha Yoga asanas, as well as for all other physical activity. The endurance, flexibility and sensitivity of the body expands as well as its ability to withstand pain, hunger, cold or heat.

At the same time, every kind of pleasure becomes more intense. All sensations are enriched with countless tints and tinges, changing the world from seeming like a bleak, black-and-white picture into a colorful, overwhelming work of art. Life itself has a new, delectable flavor.

One day I stopped to visit a former school mate. There was a birthday party going on at his place, and everybody was drunk. From the time that I first came in contact with the flow, I had lost my interest in alcohol, although I scarcely could have imagined living without drinking before. Once I took a sip of vodka, but instead of pleasure I experienced a disgusting sensation and a sense that I was poisoning my body, but I also immediately felt the flow rushing in to purify my blood. It seemed such a pity to be wasting this priceless energy on ridding myself of toxins that I have never indulged in alcohol since.

But what was I to do at this party full of drinkers? I was just about to practice the "shadow" technique and simply slip away, when I caught sight of a guitar hanging on the wall. Something urged me to pick it up.

I tuned the guitar and started to play. The people gathered round me and took up the song. It was an old Russian vagabond tune fit for a full Slavic chorus. I am not much of a singer, but it felt like I had struck home. The flow became intensified, as it always does when a conduit is opened for it, but what happened next caught me by surprise. There were no singers or musicians among us, but our amateur chorus, raucous and discordant, grew more and more harmonious as we sang. Eventually our voices, as though conducted by an invisible, masterful, harmonizing power, blended into a crystalline polyphonic order. We sounded so majestic that we couldn't believe our own ears. We felt elated and transported. The experience was overwhelming. We listened to ourselves, struck with wonder.

I was becoming accustomed to being surprised in those days, yet this was the first time I observed the flow working through me in a group of people. I could see the effulgent rain of energy entering us and somehow affecting our vocal cords. When we were done, tears welled up in our eyes, sparkling with amazement. Everybody sobered up. When I was taking my leave, one of the guests exclaimed, "It was as though somebody was knocking at the door. Thank God, we opened up."

The flow changes the very perception of the body. You stop thinking of it as mere flesh and blood. The body becomes light, transparent, and imbued with an invisible, volatile fire. It is this same inner fire, known as "Thumo" among the Tibetans, that allows highland yogis and hermits to survive unclad in eternal snows.

On many other occasions, curious phenomena emerged spontaneously. Nelli had a run-down tape recorder which we used a lot. Any serious spiritual discipline, especially when performed in a polluted urban environment, requires a repeated purification of the place of practice. Sound, fire and incense are the basic external means for such space-cleansing. To this end, we used the tape player to keep music going most of the time. The sound quality of the tape recorder was very poor, but as we couldn't afford another machine we had to put up with it. One day we noticed that the tape recorder began working better. We didn't take much heed of it at first, but the clarity and the range of the sound really did keep on improving, and, in a few days, the tape recorder sounded like a sophisticated machine. It became our little home miracle. Nobody who happened to hear the recorder play could believe that the inside of the machine had not been completely revamped. The hi-tech wonder didn't last long, however. Having given out the best it could, one day the tape recorder conked out completely. No doubt, the overabundant energy of the flow had blown its circuits. Needless to say, its demise was a death of honor!

The flow considerably impacts the perception of time. Life in the flow becomes exceedingly eventful, brimming with both inner and outer events. Due to its intensity, a day in the flow seems endless and psychologically is the equivalent of weeks or even months of ordinary life.

Such time compression Tausha called "fighting the time." He pointed out that any true spiritual practice has just one actual meaning—shortening the time of human suffering. Considered from the perspective of spiritual work, the evolution of man as a species no longer depends on his survival skills. It solely depends on the timing of his comprehension.

Widening the limits of perception far beyond the ordinary is a striking feature of the flow. Once loose, unfettered perception is no longer confined by the boundaries of the material world. The flow discloses itself as a bridge connecting worlds and times.

Being merged in the flow is like soaring in the ever fresh eternal wind that blows through all realms of existence. The only barrier that limits the flight is the fear that unmistakably marks the boundaries of one's readiness for further exploration. In other words, this readiness is defined by the energy level of the seeker.

Living in the flow puts an end to loneliness, since the current manifests itself as an all-embracing Presence. You feel as though you are being supported by a mighty hand, stretched down to you from above. The flow becomes a most intimate and encouraging friend whom you can always lean on and who is ever by your side.

Tausha did not let us forget, however, that apart from marvels and wonders, dealing with the flow is an arduous labor, demanding complete attention and sincerity.

The most difficult aspect of the task is to stay detached from the flow's fruits. If Tausha observed any of us sliding towards enjoying the energy or whatever was brought into our lives by means of it, he admonish us saying, "Don't grasp!"

Still, we were young and hungry. How could we stop grasping?

18

When a man cannot learn the truth through wisdom,
he has to be taught it through suffering.

What was the source of the flow? Where was it coming from? Tausha would invariably point to Shambhala as the source of the "green beam," but this still sounded like never-never land or at best, sacred mythology, and the whole matter remained a conundrum to us. Only once, when Tausha, Nelli and I were alone in the apartment, did the master give us a concrete account of Shambhala.

In Sanskrit "Shambhala" means "the source of happiness." Shambhala is a mysterious country hidden behind the snowy mountains north of Tibet, ruled by an assembly of enlightened sages. In the Russian mystical tradition this region is called The White Waters because of a salt lake located within it. Long ago, these sages, or Mahatmas (which in Sanskrit means "Great Souls") had been ordinary men and women, who reached the Sacred Land as a result of their spiritual quest. The Mahatmas live simultaneously in two worlds: the objective world of matter and the celestial spiritual world, and it is through them that our planet is connected with the higher realms. These sages, who have already accomplished their evolution on this planet but have chosen to remain with humankind to facilitate its spiritual progress, are the guardians of the Earth.

Upon finishing his account, which took about an hour to deliver, Tausha remained in silence for a while. It was then that we saw the flow with our physical eyes for the first time. It manifested as a conical shaft of greenish light, shining with its broad end down, and, all of a sudden it was here, covering us like a cap. The shaft was effulgent with a streaming emerald glow, and to be situated under it was to be bathed in the very essence of bliss.

Have you ever watched the dust play in the sun rays in a dark barn? The shaft looked exactly like that. I stood up and stepped out of it for a moment. The blissful sensation was gone! I stepped back in and it returned. I experimented entering and exiting a few times. The result was always the same—within the resplendent cone I felt an intense delight that ceased as soon as I stepped out of it. Tausha and Nelli sat there motionless, a faraway look in their eyes. All conversation ceased, as words had become meaningless.

It struck me that the truth has to be experienced with every cell of one's body, not just grasped mentally or even emotionally. The effulgent flow was a ladder we had to clamber up, using our bodies as a compass in search of direction.

During this period, our group was growing. I myself was very actively recruiting new people—Tausha even called me his "personnel department."

Some new members, once they joined us, just couldn't tear themselves away from our place. One such person was Michael, a musician, who dropped by one evening when Tausha was away and stayed until "metro time," the time just before 1 a.m. when one had to leave to catch the last metro train. Michael was an extremely sensitive person of a light constitution, an "ethereal type," as Tausha put it. He had been practicing yoga for a long time, trying to deal with certain health concerns but to little purpose. He was very compassionate by nature and he picked up the flow right away. Michael, incidentally, is the only man I know who married a disabled person. His wife had lost her leg as a child in an accident.

He lingered, as I mentioned, until "metro time," asking the same question again and again: "What's going on around here?" At last he left, intending to come back the next day, but around 4 a.m. we were awakened by the doorbell. There was Michael, dressed in his pajamas under an unbuttoned coat, barefoot, his face chalk-pale and hands shaking.

"Do you have an icon?" he blurted out.

I let Michael in and led him to the "red corner," the place in a Russian home where an altar is kept. In our red corner there was an icon of St. Panteleimon the Healer, belonging to Tausha. Michael knelt down before the icon and began crying.

Everybody woke up. The poor fellow did not answer our questions but just kept shaking and crying. Tausha was out of town, Michael was apparently going crazy, and none of us knew what to do.

Later, Michael told us that he had having arrived home in a high-spirited mood, got dressed for bed and had begund telling his wife about our group when, out of the blue, he was set upon by an invisible, hostile force. Michael started losing control. He sensed that stark madness was advancing upon him, so he rushed out, hailed a taxi and came back to our place in total delirium, seeing weird visions and hearing threatening voices that gave him preposterous orders. In one of the visions he saw a huge field full of people, each of whom represented himself in a different previous lifetime.

On the spur of the moment I decided to try the old traditional method for dealing with demonic possession: dousing the victim with cold water. We filled two buckets with icy cold water and gave Michael a good shower, chanting protective mantras at the same time. It helped somewhat. Michael fell asleep, but in the morning the madness was on him again. Michael now imagined he was a dog, and he crawled around on all fours, barking. He even tried to eat from the cat's bowl in the kitchen.

About noon one of my patients showed up. She was a respectable lady of a distinguished social position. I told the others to coop Michael up in one of the rooms until the patient left, but while the lady was chatting with me about her concerns, Michael broke loose. He rushed by the patient on all fours to the cat's bowl, snatched something from it with his teeth, and withdrew in the same manner. The lady appeared to be transfixed with horror. I made an effort to put a brave face on a sorry business.

"Don't worry. That's just an in-patient of ours," I said as soothingly as I could.

"Are...are you dealing with cases like this?" asked the lady in a broken voice.

"Oh, yes," answered Tausha instead of me, suddenly appearing at the door. A short silence came over us. The lady was obviously in a pickle. She stood up. "I'm sorry. I guess, I ought to leave now. We'll have a session later sometime."

After she had gone, the domicile was rent with gales of Homeric laughter. As soon as our excitement died down, John adressed Tausha seriously, "Whom the gods would destroy they first make mad. What are we going to do about Michael?"

"Don't worry," the Chief said reassuringly. "He'll make it. Call his wife and tell her he'll be back soon."

Michael, however, did not recover immediately. He remained a dog for several days, until one night when we were aroused by the sound of a body falling. Michael was lying on the floor with a kitchen knife sticking out of his belly. Blood was running out of the wound but Michael was definitely alive, for he was gasping for breath, though he was unconscious. There was a note on the table which read: "May the one who has fallen arise. May the one who has taken flight not fall again!"

Luckily, the knife was a blunt one and hadn't penetrated to his stomach but was just stuck in his abdominal muscles. Tausha put a bandage on the wound and commanded, "Everybody out of the kitchen! Keep the door shut and don't let anyone in!"

The two of them stayed in the kitchen for more than ten hours. When they both came out, Michael looked utterly transformed. He seemed somewhat stupefied, but at the same time was positively radiating glee. We gathered round the reborn Michael, touching and hugging him.

Tausha sat down in the armchair and lit up a cigarette. He looked bushed. Without answering our questions, he just commented, "Some exercising in exorcism."

Then Tausha took off his sweater and handing it to Michael, said, "Put this on. It's going to be your chain mail for a while."

We did not know at that time that a piece of clothes can work as a protective shield.

Later, Michael told us about his experience while Tausha had been working on him. He said it felt like being turned inside out under piercing beams of light coming from Tausha's eyes.

Shortly afterwards Michael joined the group. His etherealness and sensitivity proved to be signs of a real aptitude for the work; he developed into an eminent diagnostician and began working as a healer.

19

Practice is not something imposed upon you. It grows out of your understanding.

One day Nana dropped in, bringing with her, as usual, a couple of bags filled with delicious things to eat. KGB employees, as well as the Communist Party elite, had access to the so-called "special shops" where they could purchase items unavailable to the ordinary person, items such as caviar or Levi's jeans. Watching us eat, Nana showered us with news, "Have you heard the story of Yeliseev's treasure?"

Our mouths were full and we could only shake our heads in the negative. Yeliseev had been a prominent Russian merchant who ran a major chain of supermarkets in St. Petersburg and Moscow at the beginning of the century. After the 1917 revolution, Yeliseev emigrated to the West with his family. The stores were still functioning, although the selection of foods was a far cry from what it had been under the original owner.

Nana continued, "A descendant of Yeliseev who lives in the U.S. appealed to the Soviet authorities claiming his rights to a certain treasure the elder Yeliseev supposedly had hidden away somewhere in the Leningrad store. You may remember that a year or so ago the Leningrad supermarket was closed on the pretense of renovation. That was actually just after the appeal was received. The Soviets rejected the claim, but they searched the supermarket thoroughly, turned everything upside down and even removed the floor, but found nothing.

"The heir contacted the Soviets for a second time, offering his assistance in finding the treasure. This time the KGB invited the descendant to Leningrad. He arrived at the store, saw the havoc wrought by the shammed "renovation," smiled, and pointed up to a gigantic chandelier hanging from the ceiling. 'Bring it down,' he said.

"The chandelier itself turned out to be the treasure: it was made of gold but coated bronze as camouflage. The supermarket was reopened soon after, but nobody has seen the chandelier since.

"And here's a current newspaper." Nana unfolded the paper and read from it, "'It is rumored that there was an ornate chandelier hanging at the Yeliseev supermarket before the renovation. The readers keep inquiring if this is true. Based on the data provided by the city Architectural Committee, we have to contradict these rumors and reassure our readers that no chandelier whatsoever ever hung at the store.'"

Everybody laughed uproariously. When we quieted down, John quoted a Russian aphorism, "If you see a tag reading 'buffalo' on the lion's cage, don't believe your eyes."

Then Nana told us of the latest KGB parapsychology work. "Listen to this! The ESP laboratory has conducted an amazingly simple experiment proving the existence of the human soul by *weighing* it. They put a dying person on the scales and checked his weight immediately before and after death. There was a difference of four grams."

"Do you think that human souls differ in weight from each other?" Seryozha asked.

"Absolutely," Tausha put in. "Moreover, they travel in different directions after death, depending on the soul's weight."

"What do you mean?" questioned Nana.

"Don't you remember those scenes of weighing the soul after death, represented in the mythologies of religions? Have you ever asked yourself why hell is down below and heaven is up above? The answer is simple: the heavier the soul is, the quicker and lower it goes down after death; and the lighter it is, the easier it takes off."

"So everything's quite materialistic?"

"Very," said Tausha with a wisp of a smile. "And what's the conclusion?"

"To make one's soul as light as possible!" John exclaimed.

"Correct," agreed Tausha and addressed Nana, "What else are our KGB colleagues working on?"

"Well, they are putting tiny supersensitive microphones into the ears of schizophrenics and recording the voices heard by them."

"Wow," I couldn't help blurting out. "And what do they do with the recordings?"

Nana shrugged, "I wouldn't know. Sort them out somehow."

"Do they classify the demonic voices according to their ranks?" Tausha quipped. The company let out a roar of laughter.

Nana went on, "Here's another interesting KGB invention: the 'Mirror of consciousness.' This thing registers brain waves and transforms them into graphic images that are then projected onto a monitor. In this way any condition of the psyche can be veiwed as a picture."

"How are they planning to use this device?" I asked.

"They're using them on psychics, Buddhist lamas, yogis, Russian orthodox monks, and so forth. While being tested, they are required to perform meditation, concentration, prayer, or whatever form of special mental activity is their speciality. The results are registered on the 'Mirror' and then catalogued.

"The idea is to use this data to recreate these special states of consciousness. Through modifying one's state by checking against a pattern chosen from the catalogue and shown on the monitor—say the state of a Buddhist lama—new neural pathways in the brain can be facilitated and, allegedly, a corresponding level of consciousness achieved.

"I spoke with one Buryatian Buddhist lama who'd undergone the test. He told me that, using this machine, he could have accomplished in three months a meditation training that normally takes about ten years."

"We should get one, here," said John.

"What for?" Tausha inquired.

"Well, to study various meditation approaches."

"Wrong. Mixing different approaches does no good. On the contrary, it can be destructive. Different types of energy fields can be very discordant to one another. As a matter of fact, most religious warfare has been based on clashes of energy fields."

"But don't all the paths lead to the same goal?"

"There's no such thing as 'the same goal.' Buddhist nirvana differs quite a bit from, say, Muslim heaven."

"What is our goal, then?" I asked.

Tausha did not reply. He just broke off, sinking into his inner dimension. It was just like him. We had no choice but to shut up and follow Tausha.

20

Perfection leaves no traces.

An ancient legend has it that when time was young, men and women were not physically divided but constituted one being, called an androgyne. The androgynes experienced no pain or sorrow, as they were complete. This is how things were until the Devil dissected the androgynes into men and women, doomed to wander the earth looking for their missing other half.

It is very rare to meet one's counterpart of the opposite gender, but when such an encounter occurs, it is a great opportunity for the spiritual progress of the reunited couple. Most of the renowned love stories in history are based on androgyne encounters.

There is a symbol in the "Kunta Yoga" that represents the androgyne principle.

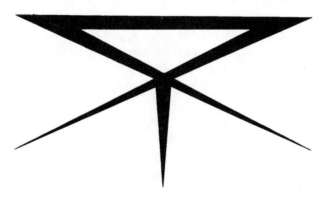

By meditating on this symbol one can increase the possibility of meeting with the yearned-for counterpart of the soul, as well as test whether someone one meets is one's second half. To do this you should visualize the symbol between yourself and the person you want to test. If it stays steady and unblurred, affixed to the individual and does not seem to want to go away, he or she is your other half.

Tausha used to sign his manuscripts and paintings with this symbol. He himself had in fact met his counterpart, but the situation turned out to be hopeless. She was married, had a child, and had no intention whatsoever of giving up her family life for Tausha's weird ways. Her name was Olga.

I saw her only once, during the first week of Tausha's and my sojourn at Felix's. She came in the morning and at the first sight of their melding auras I felt myself melting away. Tausha and Olga were obviously made for each another. I could barely stand the dazzling poignancy of seeing them together, so I served them tea and left.

Tausha didn't like being questioned about Olga, so I never did. I just felt that the whole framework of their relationship was tragic and that nothing could be done about it. Tausha did volunteer, however, that androgynes have a name in common. Their shared name was Dion.

An interesting account of an androgyne encounter was given by Nelli's uncle Ivan who had lived for many years in China. On August 6, 1945 (the day of the bombing of Hiroshima) he was having an early morning stroll on the Yellow Sea coast near a Chinese fishing hamlet. All of a sudden he stumbled upon the naked body of a seemingly drowned person, lying prone in the muddy waters. Ivan turned the body face upwards and carried it onto the shore. When he looked closely at the unfortunate person, he was stunned. It was neither male nor female, but a sexless, sky-born human being of astonishing beauty, with long black hair and a stunningly built body. The creature looked as if it was asleep.

Raising the androgyne with his arms, Ivan found it to be practically weightless. He brought it to the hamlet. The villagers were very pious people and, after a deliberation, resolved to secure the celestial creature by locking it in the barn. Meanwhile, a messenger was sent to the local monastery to call the monks for advice.

The monks arrived but to everybody's surprise, when they unlocked the padlock and entered the barn, they found the building empty. Later that day the news of Hiroshima's devastation arrived. The monks stayed at the hamlet for three more days, working out a solution to this mystery. At last they came up with an understanding. The monks said that the atomic explosion had shaken not just the sphere of the Earth but the adjoining worlds as well, including the androgynes' heaven. As a result of this shock, the androgyne had fallen from its realm onto the Earth, where it had taken human-like form. Having recuperated after the disaster, the androgyne returned to its world.

Later the faithful fishermen erected a small shrine at the site of

Ivan's encounter. At the time of Mao's "cultural revolution" the shrine was ruined.

During the seventy years period of Communist rule, thousands of Russian churches and monasteries were similarly devastated. I often asked myself: What does a nation that destroys its temples deserve? The answer would invariably come: What you see around you. And what I saw around me was a far cry from an androgyne heaven. It was, rather, a Socialist hell.

The two worst things in my personal experience with the Soviet regime were the horrible caged-in feeling of living without the slightest hope of seeing the rest of the world, and the ban on information with its corollary: heavy political brainwashing.

Back in 1980, nobody in the Soviet Union could imagine that in eleven years the empire would fall apart and Russia would become a free country again. Then, the murky colossus seemed invincible.

My grandmother was a typical product of the Soviet system—a narrow-minded atheist, though good-hearted and an eager-beaver. It goes without saying that she had nothing to do with mysticism, so I was struck by what happened one day when I was taking a ride on the metro. My grandmother had passed away some months before. As I mentioned earlier, the metro is far from being an auspicious place for meditation. Nonetheless, I couldn't help going into myself in search of new inner horizons whenever I had the opportunity, particularly since I had been introduced to the flow. While contemplating, deep within myself, I cast a casual glance through the car window into the rushing darkness outside, and was startled to see my grandmother standing there, with her hands stretched out, beseeching me longingly. But something was very eerie: though the car was streaking at 40 miles per hour, she seemed to be frozen there absolutely motionless, as if moving along with the metro just outside it! At first I was unable to make out what she wanted from me. Then I realized that my grandmother was begging me for food. She was starving. But it wasn't physical food that she wanted. She craved my energy.

She was imploring me in such a piteous and humble way that I was very moved. I felt how badly she needed my energy to make things easier for her in the underworld. She was my grandmother, and I had loved her. I was about to attempt to transmit energy to her, when suddenly I saw she wasn't alone. A whole throng of similarly hungry creatures was lurking behind her. They were also stretching their hands toward me, ready to join in the feast. I suddenly realized that I had somehow opened myself to the realm of what the Tibetans call the "hungry ghosts"! Had I given so much as a sip of my life force to my grandmother, I immediately would have been drained to the last drop by her and the starving mob that was with her.

Despite the immense compassion I felt towards my grandmother, I had no choice but to resist her plea. The hungry spirits were seeking to hook up with me, attracted by my pity. Resisting them, however, was not a simple matter. The creatures were already forming a circle around me and I felt myself being pulled into it. I had fallen into their trap. The metro car and the people around me were beginning to fade away.

I began concentrating on Tausha's right palm. He had given me that technique as a last resort to be used when in this kind of danger. Suddenly it occurred to me that the whole affair had become possible only because the hungry ghosts were able to see me. Meditating on the metro had increased the luminosity of my aura, which had enabled the spirits to perceive my energy. All I had to do to escape the ghosts' vision was to decrease my energy field's luminosity. The only way of doing this was to refocus my attention on something in the oridnary world. A passenger, sitting across from me, was reading a newspaper. The paper, from my vantage point, was upside down, so I had to summon an unusual amount of concentration to be able to read it, pulling my energy from the realm of the Hugry Ghosts back into the metro car. It worked. As my luminosity diminished, the spirits lost sight of me, although I was still able to see them with my peripheral vision. The ghosts looked rather confused and angry, trying to rediscover their fled game.

I still remember what I read in the newspaper. It was a headline: "The Soviet working class people are always ready to lend a hand to their starving brothers."

21

By making the way joyful, you shorten it.

All magic is based upon this principle: *belief in the inevitability of whatever you have deliberately premeditated, insures that it will occur.* Such belief is not an intellectual matter, but the ability to affirm a thought intuitively, without being distracted by second thoughts and doubts.

A karate master told me once that before he moves his hand to break a brick, he sees the hand cutting through it. That is to say, *it has already happened* in his mind, and the body just follows the pattern.

On another occasion a Russian folk healer shared with me the secret of his healing amulets. In the Russian folk healing tradition the charm is put into action by whispering the words that are written on it. The healer said that what the words say does not matter. Once he tried putting swear words in place of the traditional sacred formula and it worked all the same. What matters is that the impulse—the intensity and conviction behind the words—actually *enters* the body of the diseased person. Tausha called this "cutting through." Certainty creates inevitability and gives you power over chance.

Acting while in the flow sometimes resulted in spontaneous energetic manifestations. One misty St. Petersburg evening Nelli and I were ambling around the magnificent St. Petersburg temple (known in guide books as the "Savior on the Blood") erected on the spot where in 1881 Tzar Alexander II had been assassinated. The temple had been under restoration as long as I could remember and was surrounded by a fence with many gates. As we were nearing the gates, a large German shepherd watchdog dashed at us from inside. Though the gates, covered with metal net, were closed, and the dog in fact was bound and just straining at the leash, the charge came unexpectedly and I instinctively flung out my hand for protection. As I did so, I sensed something shoot out of my hand and pierce the dog. The energy blow was so strong (beause of my fear, I suppose) that the dog leaped in the air and smashed into a stone wall. He was terribly stunned, and when he recovered after a few moments, he cowered with a whine and tried to hide. Both Nelli and I were left speechless. The power of the flow we were dealing with was no innocent thing!

When we came home, we found Tausha leafing through a book. (This, in fact, was his way of reading. He could finish a two-hundred page tome in fifteen minutes and be able to recount the contents in detail.) We nervously reported to the Chief what had taken place.

Tausha tore himself away from his book and said, "Don't play around with energy. It harms more easily than it heals." Then he returned to his reading.

On another occasion, operating in my role as the "personnel department," I was visiting a former schoolmate and doing my best to enlist him in our work. The man listened to me attentively but seemed doubtful. His wife and sister were present, as well. Though he was intrigued, he felt he could not bring himself to let go of his personal freedom to pursue some nebulous "work" under somebody or other's command. I knew the predicament all too well myself. It seemed to me that to win him over I needed to do something more than articulating my arguments.

As we had just finished our meal and there were some dirty glass dishes left on the table. We were sitting in the kitchen, and there was a sink about ten feet away. Something came over me. I picked up the dishes and began throwing them into the sink, one after another. Not a single piece got broken. I felt so confident of my power over the dishes that I decided to repeat the experiment. I came up to the sink, took the dishes out, returned to my previous place and threw them back into the sink with the same result.

I was quite excited at my feat, and, riding my high horse, couldn't understand why the family didn't at least break out into applause, let alone immediately abandon all doubts regarding what I had been trying to convey to them! But they looked both intimidated and not a little disgusted. At last my schoolmate regained his composure and said firmly, "No, we are not going to join your group. Period."

It was an honest answer and I appreciated it despite the fact that my mission had ended in failure. I did not ask what lay behind my schoolmate's refusal, but the reason why some people reject and detest such energy manifestations is now obvious to me. They either thought that my whole display and thus the special energy that was behind it was inspired by the Devil, or that our whole group belonged in the nuthouse.

When my pleadings and in particular my demonstrations failed to create conviction, I tended not to dissuade my audience from thinking the worst—first of all because I must say it was fun, but also because I was not quite sure myself who or what was standing behind it all. In that particular case, anyway, I couldn't help enjoying the flying saucers.

Tausha used to work with people in a different, more refined manner. Once he was serving tea to two men. Having poured the tea, Tausha said quietly, "If you finish this tea with me, your life will never be the same." One of the men put his cup aside and wouldn't drink another drop. His life continued to follow along the same track it had been on before. The other fellow drained his cup. He was John.

Among the many things Tausha taught us, one of the most amusing and enjoyable was the sending of "magical messages." These were small pieces of paper with short hieroglyphic formulae written on them, composed to obtain intended results. We did not have the time to learn the entire Set language, so Tausha only taught us its phonetic structure and the method of writing the hieroglyphs, so that we could use them to spell out the words of any language phonetically.

Here is an example of how the hieroglyphs look.

One day a patient of ours named Tanya came to Nelli's all in tears. She was a poor and despondent single mother with three kids who had been trying for ten years to exchange her one-room apartment for more adequate living quarters. Soviet townsfolk lived in apartment buildings that belong to the state. They werer not allowed to buy or sell their apartment, but they could exchange it if they could work out an arrangement of some sort. The apartment exchange business was a whole ugly world in itself. Sometimes people managed to build up long chains of apartment exchanges in order to acquire the one they wanted. Most of these chains tended to collapse, as had recently been the case with Tanya. The deal depended on a corrupt official who wanted to have his palm greased, but Tanya couldn't afford the bribe.

So here she was, crying in despair. Tausha took out a small piece of paper with rounded corners and measuring about the size of a business card, wrote some hieroglyphs on it and handed the message to Tanya. He said that she would have to show the paper in a casual way to the official, perhaps mixing it in with some other papers. All that mattered here was that the clerk actually *see* the hieroglyphs.

A couple of weeks passed and we were already beginning to forget about Tanya's quandary. All of a sudden she showed up smiling and carrying a bouquet of roses for Tausha. Recounting her visit to the official, Tanya could not help laughing. Upon seeing the message, which Tanya had attached to her purse, the clerk not only signed all the necessary papers, but started flirting with her and ended up inviting her to the movies!

When we first began using these "magical messages" I thought that their effects might have been merely coincidental. But as time passed and we scored many successes, I had to admit that no matter how silly it seemed, the messages worked.

Tausha often used them for medical purposes. For instance, to stop a toothache he would put a tiny message, written on a piece of rice-paper, on the afflicted tooth. It worked the same way for a headache.

The real trouble began when the Chief dispensed some rice-paper messages to a woman be used as birth-control pills. The messages were supposed to be ingested before having intercourse. Since they proved effective, there was an ever-increasing stream of women yearning for these small pieces of paper covered with strange scribbles.

I cannot say that Tausha was a kind person beyond measure, but there were no personal enemies of his that I was aware of. Except one—a warlock nicknamed Varavera, who had a large following in Moscow. Rumor had it that Varavera was capable of performing various magical tricks. He was also known for enslaving numerous women by healing them through sex. Once a few ruffians assailed Varavera on dark and narrow street. Varavera lured them into a semi-dark doorway, where the thugs closed on the sorcerer and thought to make short work of him, but Varavera suddenly began to "swell," and, in the twinkling of an eye, crushed the ruffians against the walls.

I never asked Tausha about the grounds of his animosity towards Varavera. It was clear to me that Tausha held the warlock to be a conscious agent of the Dark Forces. What was more surprising was that Tausha had never actually met Varavera physically, but they had become acquainted on another plane.

Once Tausha manufactured a magical message and asked Andrew, a member of our group who happened to be about to go on a trip to Moscow, to hand the message to Varavera. Andrew was instructed not to speak with the warlock by any means, just to deliver the message and take off.

When he arrived in Moscow, Andrew found out that Varavera had recently been arrested on suspicion of witchcraft and condemned to 15 days forced labor—the minimum term of confinement in the Soviet Union. It was a very mild punishment.

The sorcerer was serving his sentence at a meat processing factory. Andrew paid him a visit there. He found Varavera with his head shaven, pushing along a carriage filled with entrails. Andrew approached and silently handed the message to Varavera. The warlock cast a glance at the message, flung it on the ground and cursed. Then he walked on his way, visibly enraged.

There was a gantry crane in Varavera's path. As he was passing under the crane, a massive metal beam fell down and landed right on Varavera's carriage, scattering its contents and covering the warlock with intestines from head to toe. Andrew just walked away, laughing his head off.

There are some rules for composing Magical Messages. Here they are:

1. The situation has to feel appropriate for intervention by magical means. In other words, all the ordinary ways for accomplishing one's purpose have to be irrelevant.

2. The message has to be brief and explicit.

3. One should be gratified aesthetically by the way the hieroglyphs are depicted.

4. The piece of paper must have rounded corners.

5. Once written, the message has to be charged with energy. It makes sense to wrap it up in foil until it is time for it to be exposed. The foil preserves the energy from dissipation.

6. The message must be incinerated as soon as possible after being exposed, otherwise it will start working the wrong way round.

7. It should be remembered that it is impossible to cast a spell on a fool laughing in a local movie theater.

While still learning the ropes, I made a message for my friend's wife Lena, who had been suffering unjust treatment from her boss at work. She wanted the boss to get laid off, so I composed the message: "Get fired."

I did not realize that I had broken rule #2 by failing to specify the name of the person to be laid off, so it turned out to be a bear's service. After Lena showed the message to the boss, which she was able to do openly and without any camouflage, he flew into such a rage that he fired her on the spot! I could only console myself that the goal of ridding Lena of her boss had been reached anyway, though the wrong way around.

The more I indulged in performing these magical tricks—Tausha taught those of us who were so minded—the more I became convinced that they are unnecessary. The real miracle, after all, was our belief in Tausha himself. This belief did not come easy to me; indeed, it was the hardest part of my discipleship. It proved extremely difficult to get myself to believe not in God but in a man. But it was this belief that made all the other wonders possible. The magical tricks, in any event, served us as a valuable training, paving the way to a more advanced practice that Tausha called "natural magic." It is a way of living wherein wonders come about by themselves without the use of any special techniques.

Life can be perceived as an everlasting magic show spontaneously unfolding in the universe, where the seats and the tickets have already been provided and all that is left to do is to watch the miracle of it.

22

Look into the quiet nature of everything.

At the end of March, 1980 we had been residing at Nelli's for three months, and it began to look like it was time leave. Nana found out that the KGB had become aware of our existence. Any one of us could be apprehended at any time. The core group now consisted of fourteen people, while the outer circle numbered about twenty associates. No doubt there had been some sort of "leak."

The size of the group was motivating us to move for another reason as well. More and more people were coming to the apartment on a daily basis. Having tasted the flow, some of them simply refused to leave! We had begun to feel suffocated. We wanted to quit the city for a while to refresh ourselves in a natural environment.

Tausha summoned all fourteen of us for deliberation. After some discussion, everyone understood the situation and agreed on leaving, but three of us would be unable to come along. Michael had to take care of his disabled wife, Konstantin was working towards his doctorate, and Nana could not quit her job with the KGB.

Where should we go? The Soviet Union was a vast country. It was not easy to pick a place to do what we wanted to do, which was to set up a tent camp. John asked why we didn't go to the Pamir mountains to see Tausha's Teacher. The Chief said that the time for that had not come yet. He said that we could go to Pamir only upon the Teacher's call and that for the time being it was a good idea for us to camp in the Caucasus mountains. Around this time I happened to be reading Osip Mandelshtam's verses about Armenia, so I suggested we go there, though none of us had ever *been* to Armenia. Tausha said that this idea sat well with him, and we decided to prepare for the trip. Tausha had lived in the woods before, so he knew what kind of supplies and equipment were required. Within a week we sold what scarce belongings we had and bought canned food, tents, sleeping bags, and other camping gear.

The last thing to arrange was to get our train tickets. Due to the shortage of everything in the USSR, it was impossible just to go out and buy them; you had to get the tickets through a middleman for a payoff. Eventually such a person was found and everything was arranged for the trip.

The morning before we were planning to depart I took a stroll to bid St. Petersburg farewell. I love St. Petersburg. It is the cultural heart of the country and the most beautiful and mysterious city in Russia, its enervating climate notwithstanding.

St. Petersburg, which was, of course, Leningrad then, had endured one of the utmost horrific episodes of World War II, the 900-day siege by the Nazis, when hundreds of thousand of its inhabitants died of cold or starvation, or were killed during the bombardments. Even today one can see the pain of those days in aged veterans' eyes. St. Petersburg still has the spirit of a stronghold, if you compare it to business-oriented Moscow. The city is traditionally a gateway to the country's North, where the Russian mystical tradition has its deepest roots.

I was walking and gazing at the city's architectural wonders, while musing about what the future might hold for our group. I myself was not yet entirely free of doubt. Unanswered questions still gnawed at me. Was Tausha really a spiritual Master or just a man of power, tirelessly experimenting with his own and his pupils' psyches? Certainly he was far more practiced in meditation than any of us. But did this justify our having thrown our lives entirely into his hands? What would be the outcome of this? Though these questions preyed on my mind, I was still very excited about our trip and anticipated amazing things to come. The general mood in the outfit, as we called our group now, was a feeling that we had just begun to live.

While I was thinking these thoughts, my walk took me to the downtown park called "Kathy's Garden," with its massive statue of Empress Katherine I at the entrance. This park is located right across from Yeliseev's supermarket—deprived of its golden chandelier. I sat on a bench and caught sight of an eccentrically dressed, hoary old woman performing some sort of ritual in front of the statue. She took off her clown-like slippers and walked barefoot onto the lawn surrounding the pedestal. Then she knelt down before the monument and started muttering prayers, at the same time manipulating something in her hands. At length she rose, put on her slippers, and began to walk around the garden.

It was a nice spring morning and a lot of people were relaxing on the benches. The strange woman gave her attention to every one of them in turn. Everyone awaited her approach. As she drew near to me, I noticed a little bag in her hand. She gave me a particularly attentive look that made me shudder, took a pebble out of her bag, threw it over my shoulder, and said, "Everything will come. Everything will come and pass." Then she walked on to the next sitter.

When I returned home, I was told that Tausha had been arrested. I could hardly believe it. Though I knew the KGB was a danger, still, I had never given so much as a thought to the possibility that Tausha might *really* be vulnerable in that way. He seemed so much the invincible warrior to me. But two KGB officers had darkened our door while I was on my walk, and Tausha was gone. Tausha, however, had not been asked to take along his personal paraphernalia—this was a good sign, since otherwise it could have meant years of imprisonment. We stayed awake until the wee hours of the morning, praying and meditating.

Thank God, the next day they released him. Tausha turned up with a sad smile and said that the time to leave had indeed come. The KGB had requested that he participate in their parapsychology research work. To politley say "no" was not, in fact, an option, but Tausha was given a few days to think it over. In the evening we left for Armenia.

23

There is negative prayer, as when one beseeches God to do as one wishes; there is positive prayer, as when the believer thanks God for what He has done. Both are based on a "give and take" attitude. But there is a third way of communing with the Forever Present. And that way is rooted in silence.

It took us three days to get to Armenia. As the train crossed the Georgian-Armenian border, the track merged into the Caucasus mountains, splendid in their anticipation of the spring's bloom. We had our tickets to Yerevan but we did not feel like going there. At the same time, we hadn't the vaguest idea where to get off the train.

As evening approached, Tausha casually glanced at a timetable and said that he liked the name of a little station called Akhtala. The outfit had no objection to getting off there, for everything we saw from the tracks was so breathtakingly gorgeous.

We disembarked from the train and found ourselves in a valley surrounded by woody mountains. Everybody was entranced by the natural beauty of Armenia. What a contrast that cozy valley was to our misty and gloomy city! The air was suffused with southern fragrance and imbued with the mellifluous hubbub of the birds.

Tausha led us a few miles up a forest road until we stumbled upon an open-sided pavilion. We decided to stay overnight there. We built our first campfire, cooked some food, and made tea. It was a feast! We stretched ourselves on our sleeping bags and talked away for hours.

The night came—so beautiful that we could not tear our eyes away from the stars. Everyone felt greatly relieved and at ease after the tension of walking on the razor's edge of Disa for the last few months.

In the morning we started our climb into the mountains. We had no map, so we just clambered willy nilly up the slope. Tausha ascended in advance. After some hours we reached a ledge that was wide enough to pitch our tents. There was a brook nearby and we set up a temporary camp. We were dead tired from the climb but ecstatic to be discovering nature anew. After all, most of us were city born, but even while we were still in St. Petersburg the energy flow had dramatically changed our perception of nature. It no longer seemed like a mere background to social existence but a communicative living being in its own right. We felt that nature itself was saturated with the same mystical energy we were experiencing as the flow. The flow, however, operated differently in the open than under tough city conditions. Back in St. Petersburg, it had been much harder and more focused, shielding our group from the inimical energies of the city . Up here we did not need that protection, and the flow became soft and velvety, fusing with the natural energy field around us.

Another night passed, deep and peaceful. The next day Tausha and John set out in search of a permanent camp site. They found a roofless ruin of a sheep-fold made of stone blocks a few miles away. The locality was excellent—the structure sat on the side of a hill overlooking a majestic mountain range; a pure crystal stream rushed below.

It took us a day to relocate the camp. We cleared the inside of the sheep-fold of bushes and nettles, pitched our tents within its dilapidated walls, and made a fire place in the middle. Our camp somewhat resembled a little fortress.

On the night of the relocation there was a major snowstorm. We found out later that there hadn't been a blizzard of such magnitude in this area so late in the spring in a hundred years. It went on sleeting for several days after the snow stopped. At last Tausha intimated that we should make a sacrifice to pacify the local nature spirits. Somebody started the stupid rumor that a human sacrifice had to be offered, the victim to be chosen from among us by casting lots! Tausha did not seem anxious to refute this bloodcurdling gossip, which jazzed us up big-time!

By now it was now raining (and sleeting) cats and dogs and we were getting soaking wet. The Chief said that everyone should pick one combustible item of value out of their personal belongings and that we would throw them all together into the campfire. So much for human sacrifice. After we performed this part of the ritual, Tausha chose five of us to form a circle on the hilltop. We chanted the protective mantra there for about half an hour but to no apparent *immediate* avail. It was sleeting even heavier than it had been before and our teeth were chattering. Five or ten minutes later, however, the sky began to clear bit-by-bit. In fifteen minutes the sun peered through the clouds, and before much longer we were enjoying a clear azure sky.

I remembered that John had once told us about an old Buryatian Buddhist lama who lived on a collective Soviet farm in the '30s. It was the time of mass purges when millions of the USSR citizens were slain or condemned to perish in Stalin's concentration camps, clergymen being among the most common victims. The collective farm, in fact, was the lama's hiding place where he was kept because of his faculty for altering the weather. He did not forecast meteorological conditions, but simply evoked whatever was necessary for the crops—sun or rain. I had not believed John then but now I had to admit that it is possible to change the weather by the power of mind.

I asked Tausha to talk to us about the meaning of the sacrifice.

"In the ultimate sense it's all a matter of learning," he explained, adding some wood to the fire. "By burning our things we've taken one step further towards the final tribute a person renders to the Absolute before liberation—the offering of him or herself. That ultimate sacrifice, which is voluntary and irrevocable, cannot be made all at once; it requires many lives to learn how to give away everything, and the practice of sacrifices such as the one we made just now is part of our training.

"In a more immediate and practical sense we have appeased the local nature spirits. They caused the storm because they were disturbed by our group energy field. Placated now by the fresh energy released through the ritual, the spirits dissipated the clouds."

"So we've simply fed them?"

"Exactly."

"Tausha, couldn't we just feed them with the energy directly without performing these rites?" asked Nelli.

"Yes, we could, but in addition to the reasons for performing the ritual I have already mentioned, sometimes it's easier to use certain patterns that have been developed through the millennia, that are rooted in the subconscious and ready to be put into action."

John said, "I read somewhere about a global food chain: plants live on minerals; animals feed on plants and are eaten by men; angels and demons eat men and finally everything is consumed by God."

Tausha laughed, "So everything devours everything and is devoured by everything. What an ugly picture of the universe!"

"But isn't it true in a way?" I interjected.

"Only partially," responded Tausha. "It's just half of the picture.

Apart from consuming, the universe concurrently reproduces itself. As for the consumption, there is a meditation technique called "devouring." You engulf mentally whatever comes up: pleasure and pain, thoughts and emotions, God and Satan, life and death. In the end you devour the perception itself along with its objects."

"I don't understand *who* devours the perception," I queried eagerly.

"That's the whole point. When this question emerges, you are on the verge of discovering your true self."

John broke in, "There might be a technique counter to 'devouring.' One could imagine oneself belching out the worlds."

"Teaching related to this does exist," acknowledged Tausha. "In certain tantric schools the outer world is considered to be projected through the eyes. According to these teachings, we do not see the world by means of light rays reflected from objects into the eyes. On the contrary, our eyes emit light rays and project the universe the same way a movie picture is projected on the screen."

Tausha paused, then added, "As you can see, the techniques are numerous, but all of them have been designed for a single purpose: to ascertain who you really are and how things work."

"How do they work?" echoed Seryozha.

"That's a good question," said Tausha with a note of true appreciation in his voice. He stayed quiet for a while, then went on.

"It might be explained in countless ways, but things would be still different from any explanation. The way they really are is far beyond mental apprehension. We cannot grasp the essence of the universe by thought, nor can we word it adequately. Things are just the way they are and it can't be helped."

"If everything is so predetermined, I don't get the point of learning, then," said John. Tausha's face had acquired a look of infinite patience.

"With regard to apprenticeship everything is much more explicit. Instead of the abominable 'global food chain,' I'd rather consider a sequence of sacrifices the Path is grounded on.

"Look, a teacher is supposed to give himself away for his disciples, and they offer their lives to him. That's a mutual sacrifice, isn't it? The disciples have people around them whom they minister to. Another sacrifice. The teacher, on the other hand, serves not only his students but the hierarchy he belongs to. Those who are in charge of the teacher have their authorities, as well. So it goes unto infinity, for there's no limit to evolutionary stages."

"Who is in command of the Light Forces on earth?" asked Seryozha.

"Jesus."

"What is the Buddha in charge of?"

"Gautama Buddha is not here. He's gone."

"You mean that He disappeared after He entered Nirvana?"

"Buddha taught that in reality he'd never come. In a relative sense he actually vanished leaving behind his teaching and his emissaries. That's why it makes no sense to pray to the Buddha. Prayer is Christ's sword. Jesus is holding the hardest responsibility possible."

Nelli asked, "So Jesus Christ is responsible for everyone down here?"

"Just for those who believe in Him and follow His path," corrected Tausha. "The chain of mutual sacrifices gives birth to responsibilities. I answer for the group. You are responsible for your patients and so on. By giving your hand to somebody else, you are supported in that very moment. This is the law.

"The arrival of the flow is the evidence of this law. The interrelated chain of mutual sacrifices and responsibilities becomes the flow's stream bed. In this sense, the Hierarchy of Light is a very fragile structure, because it's based on surrender, not on constraint. If just one link in the chain gets destroyed, the current stops running any further. As soon as the ego gains the upper hand, everything may go to hell but..."

While drinking in Tausha's words, we noticed a few cows grazing on a distant slope.

"There must be a village nearby," concluded the Chief, pointing to the herd.

Left to right: the author, Seryozha, Nelli, Nelli's daughter Anna; Armenia, Spring, 1980

Playing "Heiki" in the Armenian camp, 1980; left to right: Seryozha, John, the author, Andrew, Tausha

Tausha, early 1980s, St. Petersburg

Seryozha, early 1980s, St. Petersburg

John, early 1980s, St. Petersburg

24

The greatest souls on earth have passed unknown.

The next morning Tausha and I set out on a search for the village as we had to replenish our food supplies. Living in nature adjusted our waking hours to a natural pattern, and we now were rising with the sun.

On the way, I unexpectedly fell into a materialistic mood. I knew it was my tendency from time to time to become bitter and incredulous for no good reason, but I could do nothing about it.

I asked Tausha, "What if the materialists are right and the only real thing is the solid matter around us and all these energies, astral beings, hierarchies, other lives and so on are just hogwash? What if there's nothing ahead after we die, just darkness and nothingness?"

Tausha was visibly pleased with the train of my thought. He said, "What I like about you is that you are Doubting Thomas all over. If there is nothing after death, you won't have a dog's chance to check it out. You'll just collapse and disintegrate, that's it.

"Only if something is out there, you might have a chance to face it. Thus, all you can do is to find the truth while you are still alive, don't you think?"

I had to agree with his logic, but a distrustful shadow was still creeping deep within myself.

We trekked an old tortuous trail through a gorge for a couple of hours until a huge fallen boulder blocked our way. I looked up and around for a bypass but there was none. I was about to turn back but Tausha prevented me. He took off his backpack, approached the rock, and started to scrutinize it closely, touching and almost sniffing it. I watched him amazed. The examination lasted for some ten minute; then Tausha gave the boulder a poke, and the rock fell to pieces as though it was a Lego construction. The sound of scattering stones echoed in my ears.

I was petrified. An odd and chill sensation was creeping down my neck. Never before had Tausha demonstrated power if this sort. I felt meek and defeated. Who was this man? Was he in league with the

Devil? Unable to answer these tantalizing questions, I had no choice but to play out my part as his disciple.

"How did you do that?" I asked in a feeble voice.

Tausha replied imperturbably, "Everything has its weakest point. Find it, and a flick of a finger is enough to make the whole thing collapse."

I made no comment. Foreseeing my further questions, Tausha continued, "Physical objects are not as solid as they look. There is a specific grid of energy lines behind each of them. These lines are luminous and vary in intensity. The weaker lines are darker. You are better off if you *see* them but just *feeling* the lines is all right, too. So the trick here," Tausha motioned to the spilled rocks, "was to pinpoint the darkest stretch of the weakest line and apply some pressure."

Once I began to reflect, my fear was gone. I said, "As far as I can see, those are weak *lines*, not points."

"That's right. The grid consists of energy lines, some of which are weaker than the others."

"If I've got it right, walking through walls would mean slipping between the weaker lines, correct?"

Tausha nodded.

"Would you be able to walk through a rock, if you don't mind my asking?" I asked, half-jokingly.

"I don't think so."

"Not enough energy?" I presumed, a bit sarcastically.

Tausha burst out laughing, "No, I just don't want to!"

His reply exhausted my questions. I picked up a stone the size of a fist and started twiddling it. The rock felt as hard as ever.

"Where are these lines? I can't see anything," I said, desperately poking the stone all over. Tausha smiled, "Never mind, it takes a while."

Suddenly, I sensed a spot on the rock's surface that seemed to feel a little softer than the rest of it.

"Try a different angle," remarked the Chief. "The angle of entry matters." Tausha glanced at me, as if assessing my level of understanding.

I moved my finger a bit and unexpectedly, as though driven by something beyond myself, I started scraping at the stone with my finger as if it were a chunk of butter. A moment later it split in two. I stared at the piece not believing my eyes.

"Wow," Tausha chuckled. "Bully for you!"

I could only whisper, "There must have been a crack in the stone..."

"Maybe," agreed the Chief. He lifted his backpack and walked on. I followed him.

Half an hour later, the trail took us to our destination. The Armenian village was quite different in appearance from Russian villages. The latter usually have one main avenue lined with wooden houses, whereas the one we were entering had crooked interlacing streets with stone houses running up and downhill.

There was nobody in sight to help us find a store. Eventually I spotted a cluster of kids playing and was going to address them, when a man in his fifties approached and greeted us pleasantly. He spoke with a heavy Armenian accent, "Hello, friends. Sorry, the children don't speak Russian. Where are you from?"

His name was Martin and he was the chairman of a collective farm— the top official position in a Soviet village. Martin brought us to his home. There, for the first time, Tausha and I encountered the renowned Caucasian hospitality. Martin's wife heated water so that we could wash and warm our feet. It was right to the point as our shoes had become completely soaked in the snow still remaining after the storm.

The whole household suspended their chores and waited on us. In a short while the table was set and we enjoyed delicious peasant food. I was surprised at the large loaves of Armenian bread which were as thin as paper and incredibly delectable.

A few neighbors were invited for the lunch. Because of our host's hospitality we could not refuse the famous Armenian cognac, favorite drink of Winston Churchill. Observing the ancient Caucasian custom, Martin proffered humerous, lengthy toasts.

What a different world this was from the city! One can dwell in an apartment building for years and be unaware of the nextdoor neighbor, whereas here we were treated as close kin just after being picked up on the street.

After lunch, our backpacks were loaded with home-made cheese, bread, and other food. We were not allowed to pay for it. Upon our leave the whole family and the neighbors walked out to bid us farewell.

If we could have only imagined then that in eight years' time this village, named Tsahkoshat, would be razed to the ground during the devastating Armenian-Azerbaijan warfare!

25

Is there a difference between an enlightened person and an ordinary one?

On our way back we talked about Zen. I asked Tausha what he thought about koan practice. He said, "Zen koans only work in the Japanese language and for the Eastern mentality. They require monastic solitude. Despite its seeming simplicity, Koan practice is a very tough method and doesn't always come off smoothly.

"I know a story about a Zen monk who was given a modern version of an ancient koan. The ancient koan is, "Stop a wild horse that is charging straight at you." The modern version of it goes, "Stop the express train coming from Tokyo."

"The monk meditated for years on that train, and one day he walked to the tracks and threw himself at the express coming from Tokyo."

"Did he die?"

"He was crushed in a split second."

I found it hard to comment. Silently, we pursued our course.

At length, Tausha resumed our conversation.

"We do not need any additional techniques. I've given you enough already. The proof of the pudding is in the eating. We just have to work away at what we have.

"No practice is efficient beyond the flow. On the other hand, the flow doesn't need any technique at all in order to enter you. It is we who need artificial means in order to restore ourselves to the lost primordial source."

I asked, "What, then, about the practices we have? Should we discard them?"

"It is actually best to do without them—if you can! But practice is a kind of game we have to play to mature spiritually. A child grows up frolicking."

He paused for a short while, then said with a note of true passion in his voice, "We practice to learn to live, not vice versa. My dream is to lead the group to the point where we will be able to live simply, without resorting to any sophisticated techniques. Life is sufficient in itself."

I asked thoughtfully, "If we do not practice, what shall we do then? Shall we just live?"

"Isn't it enough?" questioned Tausha in reply.

"I don't know. We must do something in life."

"Don't you think that before we start doing anything we should learn to live?"

"Aren't we living already? What should we learn about it?" I questioned.

"Are you content with your life? If you are, what's the point then? Just keep on living and it's all right. If you're not, which is obviously the case, then practice. By the way, simply drifting with the flow is the highest and the most difficult practice of all."

I made no remark for some time and then asked, "What impedes this drifting?"

"The violation of the flow's laws."

"What are these laws?"

"You actually know them already. Just try to formulate them," said Tausha.

"*Don't grasp the flow,*" I guessed.

"Almost. But you've got hold of the wrong end of the stick."

"Well, I gather the first rule is to do what the flow is given for. And since it's not bestowed just for our personal realization, we have to channel the flow to others and grow together with them."

Tausha bowed in approval, "In short, *pass the flow on.* What else?"

"Not to use it for gaining one's egoistical goals."

"That's implied by the first law. If you try to keep the flow for yourself, you are unable to pass it on. What is the second principle?"

I racked my brains. "Well..."

"If you are giving all the time, what happens then?" Tausha prompted.

"I guess you begin receiving."

The Chief nodded and improved upon my formulation, "*Keep receiving.* This law requires attention. If your attentiveness to the flow becomes steady like a trickle of oil being poured from one vessel to another, you'll inevitably reach the source of it. What comes next?"

"The flow weakens if I lose my way and strengthens when I stay on target?"

"Exactly. *Take the flow as a Teacher.* This is the third law. On this account I call the flow 'the action corrector.' As soon as one goes astray, the current cuts off."

"Is there a fourth law?"

"The fourth law says: *Go upstream.* In other words, aspire to the flow's origin."

I intervened, "Isn't it at variance with what you said before about drifting with the flow?"

Tausha smiled. "You know, an ancient symbol of Yoga is a candle flame reaching out for the sun. Do these two flames contradict each other?"

He paused a moment, and I had no urge to fill the gap. Then Tausha picked up again. "The next rule is what you mentioned first: *Don't force the flow.* This one is about patience. The mill of the gods grinds slow. The flow is a mercy bestowed on us, and we musn't snatch it out of the hand that gives it. We have to let it work its way through us into the world."

"I would add something about giving up."

Tausha nodded. "I agree. Let's put the last law as *surrender yourself.* The more we learn how to yield to the ultimate power, the more we are supported by it. This is a paradox, despite its seeming obviousness."

"Why do you say it's a paradox?"

"The flow enhances everything in ourselves including the ego, whose trap we can easily fall into. The paradox here is that while becoming stronger we must manage to reduce ourselves to ashes. Strength eventually turns into an obstacle. A powerful ego develops a kind of shell which, in the long run, closes off the flow."

We reached the boulder Tausha had destroyed earlier and stopped to take a rest. I sat on the ground looking at the rock's debris. I was about to start airing doubts once again about how he had really demolished it, but Tausha read my thoughts and gave me an understanding look. We broke out laughing together.

"I'm sorry," I said, catching my breath, "for being so doubtful."

"I don't see anything wrong with being doubtful. In my opinion, being skeptical is far worse. If you feel skeptical, you should look at the prana."

"What do you mean?"

Tausha sat down beside me. "You can see prana anytime. It's all around you in the air."

"But prana is invisible, isn't it?" I asked.

"Look at the sky," he demanded.

I shielded my eyes with my hand and looked up.

"Relax your eyes. Don't focus," Tausha instructed. "What do you see?"

"I see little transparent round things floating in the air," I reported.

"That's prana."

"But anyone can see them." I said, a trifle disappointed.

"Yes," replied Tausha calmly.

"What about at night?"

"At night look at a naked body."

"What?"

"Look at a body in the dark and you will see for yourself."

"I'll try it."

Tausha got up. "Let's go now."

"Wait a minute, I'm thirsty." There was a brook running by and I began to quench my thirst.

"A person drinking from a spring never knows whether the water has been poisoned by a dead animal upstream," said Tausha with a gentle melancholy in his voice. I spat the water out, "Are you serious?"

"Just kidding," he said with a laugh. "This is your koan for the day."

I dismissed him with a wave of my hand and kept on drinking.

26

You were free, you will be free, you are free.

Our camp life went on. The daily chores were simple and organic. Collecting wood, making fire, and fetching water were more pleasures than labors. At night, when we sat around the campfire, our conversations were far-ranging, delving into the mysteries of the universe. A great deal of self-examination went on as well. Whatever the future might bring, we were discovering happiness in the present. We felt complete, and the presence of God was settling over us.

But we *were* in a hinterland—the village of Tsahkoshat, where we went for supplies and where Martin lived, was about a three hours' walk away. (Distances in the highlands are measured by walking time, not by kilometers or miles.)

On one of our visits there, Martin suggested that Anna, Nelli's daughter, might stay with his family for a while. Nelli accepted the offer and from then on went to the village a few times a week to see Anna.

Occasionally we saw a shepherd climbing up or downhill along with his cattle and dogs. Armenian shepherds do not speak Russian, so we had to make do with sign language to get some milk.

One evening I was playing the guitar, sitting on a rock in the middle of the stream that ran beneath our camp; its music mingled with the rumbling of the rushing torrent. Nelli was doing her laundry on the shore.

Improvising on the guitar has been one of my favorite ways of practicing Disa. If you start to premeditate what you are about to play next while improvising, the whole thing is ruined. The trick is to let go of your fingers so that they move as *they* wish, not as *you* wish. If you succeed in that, you end up listening to yourself playing as though from the outside.

When I finished playing, I looked at Nelli and thought that laundering might be as good a practice as guitar playing. I was going to say that to her and extended my arm towards Nelli to catch her attention, but as I did so, I suddenly sensed that I was actually touching her, as if my arm had prolonged itself across the few yards that stretched between us. Nelli sensed it too and uttered a shriek.

What a remarkable experience it was! I put the guitar aside and kept touching Nelli, her laundry, the rocks, the grass—whatever I could reach with my energy feelers. The world of matter in its solid state had apparently fallen away! The phenomenon only lasted for a few minutes, but it was enough for me to realize that our faculties of perception and even of action are potentially limitless.

Though I was in raptures, Nelli did not feel quite at ease after the experience and seemed a little bit flustered. I got the idea of giving her a pacifying massage. We went into the tent. While working on her back, I happened to relax my eyes and noticed that her body was clouded in a dim shimmering light. It was dark inside the tent. Numerous tiny white and blue stars, glittering here and there on Nelli's back, made her body resemble a clear night sky, blanketed with constellations.

An ancient analogy between the human body and the cosmos flashed into my mind. The sight was so mesmerizing that I stopped working. I recalled what Tausha had said about seeing prana at night. Seeing the body shrouded in a faint pulsating silver light was even more startling than my vision of the prana particles floating in the air.

Some of the small lights flashed brighter than the others, as if they were sending cryptic messages to me. I realized that these lights were actually located at acupuncture points on Nelli's back, so I started working on them in a sequence following the flashes.

In the course of the massage it became clear that the lights were indeed delivering messages from Nelli's body indicating the most beneficial combination of acupuncture points as well as the optimal succession for working on them. It was the wisdom of the body at work. Later we frequently tested this method (which I called "the massage of the flashing points") on ourselves and our patients. It proved to be very effective. On one occasion, I tried to heal a member of our group, Andrew, who was sand-blind and whose personal history before he joined the team was quite unusual.

Andrew had been a very ordinary student at the Technical Institute and, at that time, he was an atheist. It was quite the thing in the USSR to send students, as well as both white and blue collar workers, to work in agriculture once a year. Where Andrew was working, the students were assigned to dig potatoes and load boxes filled with potatoes onto a truck. One day, Andrew had just handed a heavy box to the man on the truck, when the man dropped the box and it hit Andrew on the head. Andrew came off with a slight brain concussion, but, besides this, something had "clicked" in his mind and he was a different person thereafter. He left his wife, quit the Institute, cut off all his contacts, and immersed himself in meditation.

Andrew's parents were on the brink of submitting their son to compulsory psychotherapy when he vanished. He reappeared after three years, having lost almost all his teeth and with very bad eyesight. He had managed to cross the extremely fortified Soviet-Chinese border, reached the Himalayas on foot, found a solitary lamasery, and was about to be ordained there. He returned to St. Petersburg to bid farewell to his parents, but a friend brought him to Nelli's, he met Tausha, and never returned to Tibet.

Andrew had damaged his eyes in a dust storm while crossing the Gobi desert and had to wear glasses with thick lenses. It occurred to me that eye problems might be treated with a curative energy ray emitted out of the healer's pupils, so I asked Andrew to sit down in front of me, take off his glasses, and stare straight into my eyes, refocusing his vision so that his pupils would gaze eye-to-eye into mine.

The energy is much easier to manipulate with the eyes than with the hands. The treatment was quick. Andrew told me later that he'd felt as if his vision had been refocused momentarily and brought back to normal. The healing effect lasted, however, for only a couple of hours. I myself experienced an acute pain in the eyeballs, which caused me to cover my eyes with my hands. When I took my hands away, I was blind as a bat.

I now consider it an extremely valuable experience to have gone blind temporarily (luckily, I regained my sight the next day). To understand what I mean I would recommend to anybody to blindfold himself for a few hours. The world becomes a different and much more appreciated place afterwards.

Because of my experience, Tausha put a ban on any further unauthorized experiments with energy, but I managed to get into a fix one more time anyway.

We practiced Heiki a lot, since the whole ambiance tempted us into motion. There was a glade on the top of the hill under which our camp sat and where we had flattened some ground for exercising.

Seryozha and I had decided to do some sparring. While we were walking up the well-trodden footpath leading to the glade, a peculiar question came into my head: was it at all possible to take Seryozha out right on the spot without using any particular technique? As a matter of fact, I did not give it much thought; the question just flashed across my mind. What happened next, stunned us both. Instantly I sensed myself being pumped up with concentrated energy. I remember a cruel school prank where nasty boys put a straw into a toad's mouth and inflate it with cigarette smoke. I felt exactly like a puffed toad! When I was completely full, I spontaneously leapt in the air, and, without any contact from me, Seryozha tumbled over, his face grown deathly pale. He was suddenly so weak that he couldn't get up. I realized that my spontaneous, and seemingly innocent question, had initiated an involuntary act of "energy-sucking"!

I rushed to help Seryozha to his feet, mumbling some silly excuses. He was unable to move, a faint smile was playing on his lips. I started shaking Seryozha, hoping to revive him. Thank God he eventually got up. "Never do that again," he said, and staggered down to the camp. Poking along behind him, I was sick at heart. This was something new. Was I turning into an energy vampire? I had heard spooky stories about babies left in their strollers by their mothers while they shopped, being killed by energy vampires who sucked the life force out of them. I took these stories for yarns—and now this!

Tausha laconically remarked on the occurrence with the Russian equivalent of "Shit happens."

27

To win the favor of the Gods, one has to become like Them.

It had been a long-standing wish of mine to see Gekhard, one of the most sacred places in Armenia, near Yerevan. John and I both asked for Tausha's permission to visit there, but the Chief only allowed me to go. No comment, no explanation—Tausha's style.

Martin provided me with a letter of introduction to his family in Yerevan. I found a "matryoshka," a traditional Russian doll, to bring as a gift, packed my backpack and left.

I arrived in Yerevan in the afternoon by train and went right over to Martin's relative. His name was Levon. To my surprise, he turned out to be an art critic, so my present was right on target. A "matryoshka" consists of a few wooden hollow dolls put one inside another. Tausha remarked once, that the "matryoshka" is a symbol of the multi-layered human psyche.

I immediately took to Levon and his wife Eve. They treated me like family, lavished attention upon me, and showed me around Yerevan, which proved to be an unpretentious and reserved town made of pink tufa.

The more I looked into Armenian faces, the more I liked them. There is a certain sadness in the dark Armenian eyes that is present as well in the long drawn-out melodies of the duduk, the Armenian flute. Perhaps both are a reminder of the long and tragic history of Armenia. Over a million Armenians were massacred in the beginning of the century by the Turks. The Armenians are Christians. The Armenian cross, with its forked and rounded ends, resembles a flower.

After two days in Yerevan I went to Gekhard. It is a cave temple, hewn out of rock by a single man—his life's work. The temple's carvings are scantily illuminated through a round opening overhead. The old priest who served as my guide through the temple pointed up to the opening and said, "That's where he started."

The Gekhard temple overlooks a marvelous gorge with a fierce torrent rushing below. The whole ambiance is permeated with the ascetic spirit of the Christianity of the old days. I spent a couple of unforgettable hours chanting by the stream. The sound of my voice blended with the roaring of the foaming torrent and I was completely at one with the universe.

I returned to Yerevan and planned to stay overnight at Levon's and take a morning train back to Akhtala. I had caught cold and was feeling somewhat groggy, but I did not abandon my custom of meditating by night. After Levon and his wife went to bed, I sat cross-legged on the couch and merged with the healing flow.

An hour later, Levon suddenly broke into the room. For no apparent reason he was boiling with rage.

"Get out of here!" he cried out. "I can't stand it any more. Out!"

I could not believe it. Levon had seemed to be the perfect image of a gentle, intelligent art critic. I automatically shielded myself by visualizing a protective symbol "IM" and got up. Eve awakened and ran into the room. I was silently but hurriedly collecting my things and packing them up to leave. Levon was totally beside himself, his hands shaking.

Shocked by the scene, Eve shouted at her husband, "What are you doing? You are disgracing our home!"

Levon retorted something in Armenian, getting more and more rattled. It looked like a frurious quarrel was brewing, so I grabbed my backpack and left.

I walked down the Yerevan streets toward the railroad station attempting to collect my thoughts. Even though I was well aware that the flow could awaken unprovoked animosity in some people, the way Levon had shown me the door was a bit extreme, and I was rather upset. I spent the rest of the night at the railroad station.

I learned later that Levon sent a letter to Martin, expressing his apologies.

Approaching the camp, I discovered the Chief rolling about in the grass. For a moment I thought he had gone mad. "What are you doing?" I hollered, panicking at the thought of the group being piloted by an utter lunatic—the blind leading the blind.

"I'm doing Disa," replied Tausha sanely enough, catching his breath. Then he got up and specified, "The bodily Disa."

"Just moving around as you wish?"

"Not only that. *I'm moving the energy as I wish*, and the body follows."

I sat on the ground and gave him a searching and slightly amused glance. "What is it for?"

Tausha answered without changing his prone position. "The bodily Disa serves several purposes. Living in the city makes us forget how to move authentically. We have all developed the habit of maintaining stiff unnatural poses that depress our psyches and prevent the energy from circulating properly. Look how you are sitting, for example. Are you comfortable?"

I had to admit that, as a matter of fact, I was not. The moment I realized that, my body automatically relaxed and took another, more restful position.

Tausha gave me an approving peek and went on. "Listen to the body and follow its impulses, for the body has its wisdom, accumulated through aeons of evolution. If you learn how to move correctly, it will shield you from many diseases, as well as fatigue and depression."

"The bodily Disa has to do with sex somehow, hasn't it?" I surmised.

"Sex is an art of motion. A forgotten art. Various discrepancies in sexual life are caused by suppression of the natural flow of body motion. People just don't let themselves move as they really want to."

Tausha waited a moment and then continued, "But the main objective of the bodily Disa is training in spontaneity. When you are moving, do not anticipate what your next movement is going to be."

Tausha made a few strange gestures with his hand.

"Unpredictable actions give us the invincibility we need to open the door of freedom. I want you to remember this well." His voice had become unfamiliarly stern.

"Disa puts an end to being programmed—an end to slavery. There are two levels of programming: a social and genetic one. We have been programmed since our childhood by society which, for the sake of its own preservation, instills in us its patterns of social behavior. It is extremely hard to get rid of these patterns, but harder still to remodel the genetic behavioral code which preserves us as a species. Do you follow me?"

I bowed. Tausha went on explaining.

"Both levels are safeguarded by fear. Society oppresses us with the terror of punishment, ostracisim, or neglect, whereas nature holds us in check by making us panic before the unknown. In order to overcome these patterns or, in other words, to de-program ourselves, we have to do two things. First, we must become aware that we are now and have always been little more than programmed zombies; second, we must evolve a new mode of conduct, a practice of unpredictable behavior."

"Do you mean to become unpredictable to yourself or to the others?" I questioned, somewhat puzzled.

He frowned. "If you don't know your next move yourself, how on earth can others find it out?"

"But this is total madness."

"Mind-less-ness," specified Tausha with apparent relish. I did not have much else to say.

28

A long time ago, there were two friends who lived on the same river, though their villages were separated by a few days' voyage. Once one of the men decided to pay a visit to his friend. After long preparations he set sail, but when he was half-way there, he suddenly realized that his desire to see his friend had disappeared. Without a hint of hesitation the man turned his boat about and returned home.

One May evening we were clustered around the campfire as usual. Our spirits were running high and there was much singing and merrymaking. Our second month in the mountains was drawing to a close. Due to our incessant training, our group energy was growing into real power, though the only one actually capable of focusing this power was Tausha. And here he was, sitting by the fire, drinking his tea and half-smiling at an anecdote (the one in the epigraph to this chapter) that he had just told us. Brooding as usual over my ever-pending questions, I sat watching him. What was he up to? What had providence ordained for us all?

Casually I shifted my gaze to the hilltop. To my horror, I saw the one being in all the world (or out of it) I least wanted to see: there, on the crest of the hill, was standing the Prince of the World.

My spirits began to sink. I sensed that old familiar chill in my heart. From my previous experience I knew far too well that there had to be a serious reason for the Prince's coming. This time He had not come for me, however. He'd come for Tausha. Suddenly I sensed a strange connection between them.

Nobody noticed the appearance except Tausha and myself—everybody else was just having fun. The Chief was laughing too. I gazed at Tausha intently, when in an instant I saw the Prince's features burning through Tausha's countenance. I rubbed my eyes. Yes, unmistakably, it was the Prince, laughing through Tausha's face! Was I hallucinating?

The Chief appeared not to be concerned at all. What was I to make of this? Now Tausha's visage seemed more horrifying to me than the mighty cold presence of the Prince himself.

Thus a period in my life of being profoundly confused began. On the one hand, I did not want to admit to any doubts about Tausha, and I was aware of how adept in the art of deception the Prince could be. To play in this way upon my own lurking doubts about Tausha might be just the cleverest trick imaginable to split me off from the group. But what if the horrible affinity I had intuited between them a moment before was real?

I accosted Tausha in a low voice, "Do you know who is here?"

He gave me a knowing look and nodded, "Yes, I do. Everybody's invited to the fire. What's the problem?" A peal of laughter from the others drowned his words, and the entire atmosphere was beginning to feel utterly demonic. A shudder ran through me and I gritted my teeth, realizing that I would have to clear up this riddle all by myself. But how?

I got up and took to my tent. Meditation was my last resort and I set to meditating in earnest, hoping to get to the bottom of what was going on; but the more I meditated, the more I became alarmed. My sense that we were all in imminent danger kept on growing. I had recruited most of the people and the responsibility for their spiritual well-being was as much mine as Tausha's. I kept turning it over and over in my mind until I was sure that I was unable to resolve my plight. I had too much on my plate. I had neither enough experience nor wisdom to clarify the nature of Tausha's relationship with the Devil. And above all, I could not discern whether I was under the power of a purposefully suggested delusion.

I summoned Nelli. She came into my tent and I shared my doubts with her. When she grasped what I was saying she blanched visibly and started quivering. She confided in me that she also felt that something was going wrong and she was afraid I was right in my anxiety. I asked Nelli to keep cool and pray with me for help. Half the night we stayed immersed in prayer, beseeching The All-wise to show us the way out.

During our stay in the Armenian countryside we had begun to forget about the demonic assaults we had experienced back in St. Petersburg. That night, however, we could not sleep, nor could we leave the tent—we had become aware of a hord of fiercely dancing, ice-breathing demons encircling our tarpaulin shelter!

By morning, we knew what we had to do. An understanding arose between us that not only did we have to leave the camp ourselves, but we had a duty to influence as many people as we could to break away.

Nelli went to the village to retrieve her daughter. I spent the whole day talking to each of the others in turn, except for the most true blue—John and Seryozha. I tried to talk everyone except them into leaving. I did it with a heavy heart, for I was now attempting to destroy our outfit, in the creation of which Tausha and I had put so much effort. At the same time, I was absolutely certain about what I was doing.

Nelli came back in the evening. Along with Anna she brought a Caucasian shepherd puppy that Martin had given her.

To my surprise, six or seven people agreed to leave. We resolved to depart the next morning and announced our decision that night at the campfire. Tausha, who had been away somewhere all day, remarked quietly, "Do as you wish."

Admiring his composure, I had underestimated Tausha's power. Had I not, we would have left immediately. Yet I wanted to stay another night to double-check everything. That was a mistake.

Tausha did not try to dissuade anyone from abandoning the camp, but he took John away for a few hours, and they did something together—I am not sure what—that resulted in everybody's refusal to leave in the morning. That was Tausha's suggestive power at work. Only Nelli and I remained resolved.

At dawn we packed our gear; Tausha counted out our share of money, and the four of us—Nelli, Anna, the puppy, and I—feeling a bit like Judases—took our hegira under the silent looks of our companions.

We walked downhill toward the railroad station through the splendid Armenian mountain woods. The sunlight streamed down loosely through the poplar and ash tree foliage. It felt airy and buoyant under the deciduous canopy. We both felt that we were being relieved of a terrible burden, and an overwhelming sense of freedom came over us.

29

A ray will not linger in the heart of the sun.

When we arrived at the station, a Yerevan-Moscow train was just arriving. The train happened to be Armenian. Of course, there were no tickets available. At first, I wanted to implement the "shadow" technique to get on the train, but we had five-year old Anna on our hands, so we ended up bribing the conductor (which was no problem at all) and got a whole compartment.

As the train pulled out, it finally sank in that the strangest page of our lives had just been turned and now we were entirely on our own. We got to the dining car and ordered the famous Caucasian shish kebab. After two months of vegetarian diet it hit the spot. The puppy shared in our gastronomical delight.

We did not want to go back to the city right away so we decided to get off at the Black Sea shore. At daybreak, we disembarked at New Aphon, a small littoral town 8 miles east of Abhkazia's capital, Sukhumi. I had been there once before, escaping a cruel St. Petersburg winter.

New Aphon is famed for its huge underground caves, Russian Orthodox monastery, and the tomb of the apostle Simon Canaanite, who established the Christian faith among the ancient Abkhazians. The monastery had been turned by the Soviets into a sanatorium, but the cave where Simon had lived was intact. It is sequestered in a magnificent canyon and has served as a pilgrimage site for two millennia.

We rented a room on the seashore and walked up to the cave after a short rest. A shabby, half-blind old man was guiding visitors around the cave on a donation basis and telling the story of Simon's life. For some reason he arrested my attention. There was something eerie about him, although I could not figure out exactly what it was.

In the evening, when we were having Turkish-style coffee at a seafront restaurant, somebody called Anna by name. We turned our heads and saw the old man beckoning to her.

"Let Anna go see what he wants," I said to Nelli.

"How does he know her name?" she asked.

"Maybe we called her Anna back at the cave." I guessed.

"But we didn't."

Meanwhile Anna had run up to the old man and brought back a big conch shell. Nelli laughed, "What a nice gift!"

I looked at the conch and exclaimed with a vehemence for which I could not account, "There must be something *to* this."

We retired late that night. The flow kept coming down on us, and so we assumed that it was not going to stop inspite of our apostasy. Following a sudden impulse, I took the conch and handed it to Nelli.

"Listen to it," I said, half jokingly. Nelli put the conch against her ear and became silent. She looked as though she had fallen into a trance. At length, she uttered in a hushed voice, "I'm getting something."

"What is it?"

"There are people out there living in the sea."

Nelli's answer made me start.

"What?"

"I can see them," she continued quietly. "They live on the bottom inside a gigantic transparent sphere filled with a kind of breathable gas that is not ordinary air. These people settled under the sea a very long time ago. They keep the seeds of the human race stored in preserve, and after cataclysms in the past have used them to repopulate the planet. This last happened after the Flood. It may happen again in the future. Their place is called the Callis. It has a connection to Shambhala but is yet quite different. Shambhala is held as a stronghold of The Forces of Light and participates in spiritual warfare on earth, while the Callis is quite a peaceful place, an incubator, where favorable conditions for human development have been created.

"The Callis numbers nearly eight hundred inhabitants. People live there as long as they wish. The corpses of those who have chosen to die are placed in cages outside the sphere and are eaten by fish.

"Occasionally they take people from the earth. Not all people who vanish into the sea have drowned! In addition, sometimes people go there voluntarily; but to remain there, they have to pass a test.

"However one gets there, once acclimated to underwater life one cannot return. The newcomers undergo some kind of operation on their lungs that makes then unable to breath earthly air anymore.

"The Callis inhabitants possess supreme knowledge, which they are eager to pass on to those of the earth people who are prepared. It is unnecessary to submerge for that. Those who are able to communicate telepathically are welcomed.

"The social structure of the Callis community is hierarchical but not oppressive. Discipline comes easy, as happiness prevails. Oh, they're so beautiful!"

Nelli swam back into consciousness and opened her eyes. Her gaze was abstracted but soulful. At that moment she seemed like a strange person from another planet to me. I stared at her incredulously.

Finally, Nelli said, "It's gone now. As soon as I saw their faces, everything disappeared."

"Do you think that the Callis might be connected with the enigma of the Bermuda Triangle? Maybe that's where they take the people away!" I conjectured.

"I don't know. I saw something like a vortex but I'm not sure. I had a feeling the whole time that somebody was speaking through me to *you*," said Nelli.

We went back to the cave several times in the hope of meeting the old man again but he had vanished without a trace.

Two days later, I was meditating alone in a solitary cove about a half mile from town. The waves were quietly lapping in between the moss-covered rocks and the sea gulls' cries were dying away in the distance.

My meditation was simply to merge with the flow. Before I met Tausha, I had tried various meditation approaches. Most of my time and energy was consumed by futile attempts to stop the drifting of thoughts, as recommended by many meditation manuals. I had merely been going around in circles and giving myself headaches, as I mentioned before.

Certainly I understood that thought cannot be caught by thought, however hard one might try. I felt that there had to be more effective means to trigger what I thought of as "The Great Change." A yearning to surrender to something greater than life was maturing in me but there was just nothing around to give myself up to, until the flow came on the scene.

Although it was given through Tausha, the flow itself is an absolutely impersonal force. That you get to feel the flow as a bridge between yourself and eternity is exactly due to its penetrating impersonality.

As I was meditating at the shore with my eyes closed, I had a distinct feeling that I was being watched. I opened my eyes. There was a man in the water, wading toward shore. He was bare-headed and had sleek tight-fitting gear on, silvery in color. When the water was down to his knees, the man halted and waved for me to follow him. Then he turned, slowly swam out to sea, and went under.

The sea was licking the rocks as peacefully as before. The time came to test my mettle. Without being quite sure that it was not a vision, I rose and stepped into the water. I waded offshore until the water became chest-deep, then I stopped. Somehow I knew that the man was waiting for me out there in the depths. I sensed his presence and was aware that he was speaking to me telepathically. He told me that in order to follow him I had to *breathe* the water. It was the test Nelli had mentioned!

The man went on to say that he was not alone; there were some others under the surface. As soon as I inhaled the water, they would do something to me so that I wouldn't drown, and they would take me with them down to the Callis. Then there followed a silence. The man was awaiting my decision.

My thoughts sped up fiercely. In the event that it was all an hallucination and I tried to follow, I would drown. But if it wasn't?

I stood there waiting, and fear started coming over me.

Feeling my hestitation, the man said, "It's yet too early for you. Come back when you are ready." He paused and then added, "You can bring others as well. If the disaster comes, you'll be safe down here."

"How would we know when the disaster is about to strike?" I questioned.

"We'll give you a sign," said the man, and with that, he dissolved into the sea.

When I got out of the water, I saw Nelli and Anna running towards me along the shore. They came to say that it was time for dinner.

We stayed in New Aphon for two more weeks. We were flat broke by then and had to return to St. Petersburg.

Once there, it was hard to get back into city ways. Andrew came back to the city a month after we did. He had some matters to settle in town. He told me that Tausha had forbidden everyone from discussing our withdrawal. But he did say that Tausha had cut off the energy channel connecting me to him.

I hardly needed to be told that. The flow, still powerful on the Black Sea, began subsiding in the city and, gradually dwindling over the next month, finally cut out completely. Whatever effort I put into my meditations, however hard I prayed for the flow to come back, nothing worked.

It was hard to believe. Living in the flow had seemed unending. I knew that the flow was a blessing, but I had mistaken it for an outright gift, unlimited by space and time. I felt like a fish plucked from the water. The flow had become oxygen for me. The world, that under the flow was like a colorful multi-dimensional panorama, was back to being its old flat, dreary, black-and-white Soviet self. I felt like I had let *real* life pass me by.

I took it as my payback for our apostasy; yet, my conscience did not prick me at all. I was still certain that we had done the right thing. But it was an agonizing energy collapse. My appetite was poor and I was having trouble sleeping. My own energy resource was as weak as a hen's tooth. The feast of power was over.

30

No doubt. No confusion. No miracles. No advice.

The group came back to St. Petersburg in the middle of July. The camp had been spotted by the local police, and everyone was driven out on the grounds that people at loose ends should go back home and get a job. Being unemployed was illegal at that time.

Occasionally I would run into Nana, who kept me posted on what was going on in the group. The outfit was expanding apace. Shortly after their return it numbered about twenty-five people. To avoid the risk of arrest, Tausha intended to set up another camp in the woods north of St. Petersburg at the Karelsky Isthmus. This region formerly belonged to Finland and is the most beautiful area in the city's vicinity. It is forested with pine-trees and spruces. Tausha had camped there alone in the past and knew already the exact place to which he was going to take people.

On the eve of their departure Tausha called me. He wanted to see me. Despite my confusion, I agreed. All in all, with Tausha's guidance I had embarked upon a journey that had no end. Besides, the guru habit dies hard. More than Tausha himself, however, I missed the broken bond with the flow that I was unable to restore on my own. At the same time, I was sure that a great battle was raging over Tausha's soul. I was somewhat hopeful that I might be of help. Our rendezvous took place at Nana's, who served us excellent coffee for the occasion.

"How are you doing?" Tausha welcomed me. He looked a bit drained out.

"Fine. Yourself?"

"All right, thank you." His voice was a little tense. "Would you like to give it another go?"

I glanced into his eyes. Tausha's gaze was tranquil and concentrated, as usual. I gathered my thoughts. Here he was, my erstwhile teacher, attempting to let me off the hook for my perfidy. Was I to beg forgiveness? Or should I go further with my challenge to him? I was experiencing deep perplexity.

"Do you know why I left?" I finally put forward.

"I guess I do."

"You will surely say that I chickened out. Well, I did. But I feared far more for the others than for myself."

"You should have spoken to me directly rather than taking it upon yourself to split up the group."

I decided to take the bull by the horns. "Why did the Prince come? He was coming for you there, or that's what I felt then. What is your actual relationship with Him?"

Tausha said with a chuckle that made me shudder, "I'm His younger brother."

I did not know what to make of this and just said nothing. It often wasn't easy to tell Tausha's jokes from his more serious pronouncements.

He proceeded, "What do you want to hear? Words don't mean much, do they? Whatever I tell you now is not going to work until you figure it out for yourself. Why not just get on with confronting the truth about what spooks you?"

Impatiently I came back at him with some fierceness, "Would you stop beating around the bush and get to the point? I *saw* the Devil standing up there on the hilltop, and now you're telling me that He's your brother! What the hell does all this phantasmagoria really mean?"

Tausha didn't move a finger. "First, it doesn't always help to deal with the big issues by becoming knowledgeable. Second, talk of the Devil and he's bound to appear. My impression is that you tend to obsess about the Dark Forces. Your own fascination provokes them into showing up. But that's not the point now. The question is whether you are going to come back to the outfit and continue the work we began, or are you really going to go it on your own."

At that moment I thought of a time near the beginning of my apprenticeship when Tausha and I were playing chess. I was a better chess player than the Chief and was about to put him into checkmate when he gave me a long quizzical look—an energy hit that put me into a state of inner confusion. He avoided the checkmate and I lost the game shortly afterwards. This time, however, I was not going to lose. I had already tasted the emptiness and frustration of being on my own without the flow and of being on the outs with the Master. But apart from that I felt I had to get to some kind of clarity about Tausha's wheels within wheels, and there was no way to do that if I remained outside the group. I consented to rejoin. My fate, however, was not about to let me return so easily. The very next day I came down with a high fever and spent an entire month bedridden.

Meanwhile, events took an even odder turn. Having set up a new camp twenty-five-people strong and made all the initial arrangements, Tausha vanished without a word. It seemed very likely that he had been arrested again. Nana made inquiries but was unable to confirm that this was what had occurred. Naturally everyone was baffled and confused, stranded, as it were, on their own recognizance; but John held down the fort, and the camp was set up in spite of Tausha's absence.

When Nelli, who also had rejoined the ranks, came by for a short visit and first brought the news of Tausha's disappearance, I could not stop laughing. In my view, it was the cleverest trick the Chief had ever performed. Nelli, however, did not share my enthusiastic but idiosyncratic spin on the event.

The leaderless camp held out until fall. The group grapevine had various versions of Tausha's disappearance, but the most popular one was that Tausha had gone to Shambhala.

From what I heard, life in the camp was not so bad. People in fact were having lots of fun. The work had ceased, however, and letting oneself go free out there in "nature" could not make up for the absence of the Master and true spiritual effort. By September many began to trickle back to St. Petersburg. Just a handful of the most determined remained into October.

About this time the Chief suddenly reappeared at my place with an enigmatic greeting: "Ah, here you are!"

After that, Tausha shut out most of his former contacts and distanced himself from all social activity, just keeping in touch with a chosen few. I was among those excluded from his now quite narrow circle of associates. The group, as we had known it, was disbanded.

31

A certain Chassidic Teacher had many disciples. Once when the Teacher was out, his students indulged in playing a game of checkers. When the Teacher returned unexpectedly, the disciples got flustered and stopped playing.

"It's all right," said the Teacher, seeing their embarrassment. "Just explain the rules to me."

The students were even more abashed and just kept silent.

"Never mind," continued the Teacher. "I'll explain the rules myself. The rules of checkers are three in number. The first rule is: a checker can only move forward. The second is: only one move per turn. And the last is: upon reaching the opposite side of the board, a checker turns into a king."

For years I have been mulling over Tausha's apparent decline. He was only twenty-four years old when the group disbanded. The burden of an ever-expanding crusade under harsh "subterranean" conditions would have been an ordeal for even a fully enlightened soul. But Tausha was just our spiritual older brother, an advanced seeker, indeed a master, yet someone who needed time and solitude to accomplish his spiritual quest. As far as I could see, working with people's consciousness involves onerous toil and a total lack of privacy, a hardship all the greater in Tausha's case when you consider Tausha's homelessness. To have an abode in Soviet society was vital. You could live virtually without money due to the easy availability of cheap food and other basics, but, with no place to live, before long you would find yourself at the end of your tether.

I also considered that Tausha was so sure of his link with Shambhala and of the righteousness of his mission that he may have thought it impossible to be deprived of the flow, and was shocked and profoundly demoralized by its departure.

In retrospect my view was that Tausha had given up his mission without foreseeing the consequences. I tried to reach him a couple of times later on that year. Once we even spent a night meditating together. But there was no heart to heart communication as there once had been. Our closeness was over.

I felt that the Prince had exacted his price. Tausha had become withdrawn and aloof, as if he had sailed off into inner space. I made no effort to get back into his good graces, and he did not call me back. Soon I lost contact with him altogether and did not see him again for a long time.

It took a difficult, interminable year for me to get back on track. That year was the most dispirited period of my life. Now I had to make my own way, and it was no picnic getting back into the world.

I felt I had gained a great deal since throwing in my lot with Tausha, but my life now, deprived of the flow, was death itself. Without the mighty current, the outside world was a far more hostile, cold and empty place than it had been before I met Tausha. I knew the occult law that states that the gates to the spiritual world open before a neophyte just enough so that he catches a glimpse of the resplendence inside, after which the gates close tightly again. Now it is up to him to reopen the gates on his own. Alas, knowing this law did not make me feel any better. I fell into a mood of reclusiveness, dark contemplation and loneliness. People, including myself, seemed to me like living corpses clad in clothes, ordained to do nothing but carry out mechanically their physiological functions.

All hope had fled and I was getting more heavy-hearted with every day that passed. I even caught myself thinking of ending it all. What upset me most was that I was blocked from the Light, and all my attempts to break back through to the Source were proving fruitless. Neither the techniques nor Disa worked. It all amounted to leaping out of the frying pan into the fire. I lived in limbo, not caring what the next day would bring.

A part of me knew for certain that it was all over, but another part was still clinging to the lost paradise, hoping against hope that someday my ship would come in. One murky winter evening, I took a lonesome walk in Mikhailovsky park, a place that I particularly loved. I was treading the snowy dark alleys, being down in my usual dumps. I pondered on how one normally acts when one is dejected. It seemed that typically what one does is to try to distract oneself from what is bringing one down. Refocusing my attention on whatever was at hand at the moment had been my own standard antidote to depression. Anything could be a help—getting myself to read, calling on a buddy, simply thinking about something else. Do anything, just *forget* about the whole thing! In short, escapism. Mere flight.

It suddenly struck me that I had to give up this practice of fleeing and do the exact opposite. I had to stop, turn around and look right into the face of my depression. So I did. And in the next moment I got to truly *see* my despair. It was a dense cloud of dark energy, hanging a little bit in front of me, above my head. This cloud was alive. I was seeing my dejection unmasked—a coagulation of dark heavy energy that had been feeding on my gloom, not only since the break up of the group, but all my life.

I opened myself and gave myself up to the cloud, taking it in. In no time a black wave engulfed me. My anguish intensified and became so acute that I began to sense it as physical pain. I had never experienced anything like it before. After a few minutes of this crescendo of agony, it reached its peak, and the pain began to drain away and subside. Then everything became empty. I felt as though I was suspended somewhere in the void, while my body continued walking. Everything became empty: the winter park, the palace looming behind the bare trees, the snow, the city, myself. This emptiness was not a black nothingness; it had a crisp quality and was filled with a certain sense of clarity. Soon this clarity started pulsating with light that grew more and more intense until the whole universe became transformed by it. The experience was overwhelming. My old sullen impotent world was transformed into a sparkling delightful symphony of light—light and joy fused into one luminous *sound,* rooted in nothing, founded on emptiness.

32

Life keeps flowing back to its source, whence there is no return.

That evening was a milestone in my life. I felt that I had stumbled onto a fundamental principle, though it took me a while to fathom its implications. My surrender to the black cloud turned out to be the clue to overcoming the depression that had been torturing me since my youth. I realized that the cloud was *my own energy* working against me because I had separated myself from it. There had been a wrong connection in my energy circuit, and as soon as it was corrected, the energy, instead of destroying me, was at my disposal. That evening I got rid of my depression for good.

As I now knew how to use the energy of dejection, I ceased from being a prey to dejection and became a hunter of life: I started to seek out the situations and circumstances that had disheartened me before. I met with people whom I used to dislike, purposely evoked discouraging thoughts and confrotned my old fears; I went places I formerly would stay away from, and so forth. However hard I tried to frustrate myself intentionally, nothing could bring me down anymore. Now I knew the secret: surrender and acceptance. Instead of being under a cloud, I was on cloud nine! Negativity turned out to be very relative; in fact, it was a treasure-house of unclaimed energy.

My victory over depression encouraged me to develop my investigations further. In the days that followed my discovery, a long chain of connected realizations followed. To begin with, before long I came to a curious conclusion: that I tended to flee not only from the negative sides of my own nature and of life itself, but from the positive aspects as well. Inwardly, I was *always* on the run. I practically never stopped to appreciate and embrace the present moment. This was a crucial discovery. It lead me to see that I was always in a state of rebellion toward both the world and myself. I rejected creation *as it is* in favor of an imaginary ideal. As a result, I kept running afoul of myself in an everlasting pursuit of change. Deeply unsatisfied with what I was and what I had, I always longed for more. In short, I realized that always running after something better was exactly what was making me lose my energy and be unhappy.

I had actually been fighting a battle against God and His creation, while thinking I was working toward perfection! Isn't that the most preposterous thing? Yet I did it with every breath. If the truth be told, both the human world in general and myself in particular are really far from perfection, so this battle might not have been such a bad thing—if I hadn't been wasting all of my vitality and stamina to fight it. But to truly work for the good of the universe and of myself, I needed the very energy I was letting slip away. Realization requires a great deal of refined energy, yet much of my priceless power had been lost in senseless confrontations. The basic nature of everything is very quiet and peaceful, but I prevented myself from seeing this by being unceasingly at odds with what simply is. The sacredness of the universe had slipped through my fingers, reduced to little more than a figure of speech.

As I worked with my new understanding, the chain of realizations continued to add link after link. I saw that I had been treating Destiny not as a friend or benefactor but as an irresistable, sly, and demanding taskmaster. In spite of Tausha's teachings I had failed to grasp that, if *my* will became united with the Will of the Almighty, obstacles in my path would be washed away. I saw that there was no other means of merging my will with the Power of the Author of all things than to surrender to It. The Will of God manifests itself through its creation. Whoever we are and whatever we have around us is that Will at work. Reading this book is the evidence of that Will, too.

I could see that surrender itself, in fact, is not hard. What *is* difficult is surrender *in action*. If we say to ourselves: "Okay, I am willing to surrender to the Lord's ways," we have only seen one dimension of the process of surrender—a single frame of a full-length movie! Only a *lasting* surrender counts, a giving up that flows from one moment into another. If we master abiding in the unceasing flow of surrender, the omnipotent Will starts its miraculous manifestation.

Most religious people I happen to have come across just pay lip service to humility. In reality they are completely absorbed in grappling with circumstances, not at all reaching out for the all-powerful Hand behind the scenes. Genuine meekness, however, has been appreciated by the sages down through the millennia, and not just because of its ethical contents. It has had to do with energy. As soon as

I quit wasting my life force on fighting with the world, my inner chalice began being filled with new energy, and this power carried me through whatever I had to face.

I also discovered what correct action is. For years I had surmised that there must be an optimal way of behaving in any circumstance, yet I could not help seeing that most of my actions had been dictated by what I thought of as a lack of energy. In fact, I had been involved in an endless search for hidden energy resources, sometimes successful, sometimes not. Even while receiving the full benefit of the flow, my own existence was like an empty barrel: no matter how much energy I was given, it all passed through me and flowed away. I had no idea how to preserve it. But now my energy chalice was full all the time and it started to brim over. A new way of acting out of opulence as opposed to acting from deficiency was asserting itself. Later, I came to call acting out of fullness rather than out of privation, simply, "acceptance."

When I formerly practiced Disa, of course I found it a very powerful exercise, and I still do, but something was definitely missing. Disa, at least as I had practiced it, divided reality into two separate spheres: the spheres of the desirable and the undesirable. The divided reality produced endless conflicts and anxieties and reinforced my obsession with encounters with "demons" and my certainty of the unavoidable reality of the Prince of the World. I had no sense of the world as a whole. But I desperately needed a sense of unity because I was positive that the world is predominatly good. The practice of "acceptance" has made it possible to live on the basis of that truth. Although I did not succeed in bringing myself back to the flow, the universe had become friendly again and my crisis was over.

33

Aspire to the Truth no matter how painful. The only efforts taken into account by the Eternal Judge are those made in the search for liberation.

A few months after my stroll in the Mikhalovsky park, I learned that I had been left a substantial legacy in my grandmother's will. It opened a door to the dream of my youth—to go into religious seclusion. It was this dream that lay behind my earlier plan to go to the Kamchatka Peninsula—a plan that ended when I met Tausha. Now Tausha was no longer around, and my dream returned. My master plan this time was to find a hut somewhere in the mountains of Georgia and to devote myself to meditation there. Since our trip to Armenia, the Caucasus mountains had been like a magnet to me.

I paid my debts and flew to Tblisi, Georgia's unforgettable capital. As soon as I arrived I knew that Georgia would surpass all my expectations. It was, in fact, one of the most affluent of the Soviet Republics. Many people owned big, beautiful houses surrounded with orchards. I fell in love with everything about the place: its old monasteries and picturesque cities, its majestic mountains, savory food, melodious music, and, of course, the people. I have never met such warmhearted, open, and hospitable people anywhere else in the world. Georgia is a Christian country and, in my opinion, one of the few truly Christian countries on the planet.

Georgians are a remarkably musical folk, and I spent my first few evenings roaming Tbilisi streets enjoying the many renditions of Georgian songs. After work, simple people would gather outdoors relaxing, drinking dry wine and singing. Georgians possess a unique seven-voiced folk singing style, and their native skillfulness at polyphonic vocal music is astonishing.

I stayed at the home of Merab Samtredia, a friend of a friend of mine. He was a mural artist and was unbelievably well-to-do by Soviet standards. The Samtredias lived in a privileged district of Tbilisi in a villa, had a swimming pool and two servants, one of whom was Japanese. What amazed me most was that Merab earned his living by painting decorative abstract frescos, not Lenin's ugly busts, like those piling up in the backyard of his neighbor, who was also a sculptor.

The Japanese servant, who went by a Russian name, Yasha, had been a student in the Russian city of Astrakhan. As it happened, he raped a daughter of his dean there and fled to Georgia afterwards, where he did odd household jobs in a prosperous Tbilisi district until Merab hired him. Luxury did not impair Merab's human qualities. This was very rare in the Soviet Union. Most affluent Soviet people were out-and-out scoundrels. Merab, however, had a rare gift of genuine kindness—he tried to help people out in every way he possibly could.

There was a small construction site in Merab's backyard. When I asked him what he was building, he said, in his lovely Georgian accent and with an enigmatic smile, that it was his old dream being fulfilled. The idea was to construct an orb, a man's height in diameter, out of plate-glass. The inside surface of the ball was to be a mirror. Merab said that he had wracked his brains trying to envisage what one might see from inside such a mirror ball. Nobody had ever been able to say what it might be like. So he decided to find out for himself. Merab joked that the ball might serve as a morning sobering-up station for his guests.

The idea enthralled me, but my path was taking me up to the mountains, and I did not have the time to wait until the construction was completed. Years later, I spoke to Merab on the phone and he told me that the ball had eventually been built, but during the civil war in Georgia in the early 1990s it was destroyed. When I asked him what it had been like inside, Merab just exclaimed, "Wow!"

Merab's wife Laura suffered from severe asthma, and I gave her a series of treatments which somewhat relieved her condition. I remembered Tausha's words, that the laying-on of hands would come in useful anywhere we went. It was really a wonderful feeling to be able to help people anytime just with my hands.

To find a good place in the mountains for my hermitage I needed Merab's assistance. He supported my commitment wholeheartedly and confided in me that my dream had been his dream as well, but he was too busy to fulfill it. Within a few days Merab provided me with a jeep and a driver, and sent me to his distant relatives who lived in Hevsureti, a remote highland area. I thanked him for his hospitality and started out.

It took a day of driving along a rutted dirt track to get to a tiny village named Shatili located deep in the mountains near the Checheno-Ingushetia frontier. I was housed at Merab's kin's place where I chanced to face an unexpected problem.

The day I arrived, a local holiday began, followed by the sizzle of unending festivity. Most of the day was spent at the table, and it was nearly impossible to resist the emcee who made me drink *araka*, a turbid home-distilled vodka. I did not know how to refuse it without offending my hosts. It was not my scene at all. I was there to meditate, not to wet my whistle. As a week of carousal passed, I came to feel like a voyeur in a bridal suite. At last, one early morning, I packed my backpack and made off.

Snowcapped peaks were looming all around the valley, and I began making my way up toward the nearest summit. Having climbed hard for several hours, I spotted a herdsmen's camp ahead. The camp sat amid snow-clad pinnacles. My heart leaped for joy. But I had been spotted, too, for a man came out to greet me with his arms outstretched. To my utter surprise and dismay, I discerned a massive ram's horn in his hand. (The ram's horn is a traditional drinking vessel in the Caucasus.) As I approached the herdsman, he held out the horn to me and said cheerfully, "Drink!"

I forced a smile and looked around in despair. The campsite lay in a dead-end glen. There was nowhere else to go, only higher up in the sky. The horn turned out to be filled with half a liter of *chacha*, a home-made grape vodka, 160 proof. I screwed up my eyes and drank it up. A fire ball went down to my stomach. The herdsman looked at me favorably and said with a wide smile, "Good!" Then I was invited to the campfire and fed with barbecued mutton.

The boon of my trek, however, came in the form of directions given by the herdsmen to a place called Mutso that seemed to match the setting I was looking for. I stayed at the camp overnight and in the morning headed out for Mutso.

Two centuries earlier, the bubonic plague had broken out in the Caucasus. Entire villages died off. Upon the first symptoms of the deadly disease, the afflicted people would leave their dwellings to bury themselves alive in specially built charnel houses. In this way, the spread of the epidemic was partially prevented.

I stumbled upon some of those houses. They looked like stone huts with a narrow opening on the side. Peering into the huts through the openings made me feel uneasy—piles of bones and skulls, mingled with still undecayed rags, were scattered inside. My mind's eye vividly pictured the wretched souls doomed to horrific death in the midst of their already dead kinsfolk and neighbors. What a mighty spirit this people must have possessed!

I also witnessed more recent touches of death in the form of modest memorials left by the trail side. These were just mounds of stones with men's photographs embedded in the middle and a bunch of empty bottles along the sides. At first, I couldn't make out what had caused those deaths. Later it was explained to me that the mounds had been erected where fiery Georgian equestrians had fallen. They loved to challenge fate by riding drunk.

I arrived late in the afternoon at Mutso. There was a canyon above which hovered the ruins of a twelfth century watchtower. I climbed it without delay. From the top of the tower I spotted a few deserted peasant houses strewn across the gorge. I climbed down, crossed the gorge, and after checking them all out, chose the most fitting one and took up residence there.

Though I had spent many nights in the mountains camped with our group, this was my first experience alone in such an environemnt. I bedded down, but the world was filled with eerie sounds that awakened my fears and at first made sleep almost impossible. I also found myself mulling over the fact that I wasn't really sure how to provide myself with the necessities for living. I had money, but there were no shops around to buy food, for example. Crystal pure water, thank God was profuse, and, lulled by the sound of a nearby brook, I soon slipped under the spell of Morpheus.

The next morning I was awakened by the thud of a horse's hoofs. When I got up and went out, dawn was breaking, the rider had gone, but there by the door was a hefty sack, apparently left by the horseman, half full of food—bread, sheep cheese, ghee, all homemade. Not bad for a start! I never found out who my benefactor was, but I was startled by the anonymous highlander's welcome. If I came, I had to eat. It was as simple as that.

34

The countless levels of consciousness exist at different distances from the Absolute, but the Omnipresent is equally close to them all.

The house was small. It was built of laminated flat rocks and had a level earthen roof overgrown with grass. I became partial to this roof. It provided a vantage point from which I could see the whole vista—the tower across the gorge, the breathtaking mountain range, the river far below.

In the evenings I would lie in the roof's grass until well past midnight. The gorge, enclosed by the dark walls of the mountains and covered with the starry sky, resembled a chalice, on the bottom of which I lay in repose. I felt like an infant at peace in the lap of the universe. At times a shooting star would catch my eye; I would watch it arc through the sky and flame out near the snowcapped range.

I lived as the spirit moved me. The ambiance was ideal for the kind of work I came there to do, but as time passed, I began to realize that things were not quite that simple. I had grown up in the stone city gorges filled with poisonous gas, and my desire to escape them originated mainly from my having read biographies of great hermits and saints. In spite of blissful hours, I was a fish out of water. It was beginning to dawn on me that my idyllic dream of being a yogi living alone with nature might be but a bookish fantasy. *My* "natural habitat" was back in the city, and I realized it might take me years to really grow accustomed to my new environment. But I wasn't quite ready to give up yet. I resolved to put myself in the hands of fate and wait to see what would happen.

One night I caught sight of a fire aloft in the distance. The blaze was so high up on the mountain slope, far above the timberline, that I knew it couldn't be a herdsmen's campfire. Intrigued, the next afternoon I packed light gear (including little more than some black Georgian tea) and started off on a climb to investigate. Distances in the mountains are illusory and, though I ascended directly, it took me well over four hours to get to the ledge where I had spotted the fire.

When I got there, it seemed at first that the climb hadn't been worth the effort. I found nothing but ashes. Who the night fire maker might have been remained a mystery. In the meantime, the sun was about to set, so I decided to spend the night on the ledge so I wouldn't have to descend in the dark. I built a fresh fire over the ashes with a few pieces of wood left by my mysterious predecessor, and brewed my tea.

Sipping my repast, I looked down the valley tinctured by the last rays of the sun. There is a certain touch of sadness in the hazy Georgian sunset, a deep melancholy that enriches the soul and melts the heart. But it was getting cold quickly, and I didn't have my sleeping bag with me so I had to find a few logs to keep my fire going for the night. The problem was that I was past the tree line and there wasn't enough fire wood to sustain a substantial fire.

As its flames began to dwindly, I sat there trying to figure out what to do, when suddenly I heard somebody call me. I turned around. There was an old man with a bronze and wrinkled face, blue eyes, and long grey matted hair. He was dressed in something that must once have have been clothes. Although there was nothing menacing about the stranger, I was uneasy. The man looked familiar but I could not place him.

I got up and we exchanged greetings. The old man's name was Grigory Veselov. He was a Siberian by birth, and a recluse—unlike myself, a real one!

He showed me to the cave he lived in, a few hundred yards away, and offered to put me up for the night. I entered the cave. It was spacious and looked rather like a labyrinth. There was a small sooty stove inside, a couple of sacks of flour, and a trestle-bed. I noticed a yellowish photograph of a young woman on the wall, and sundry tattered books on a straw mat.

Grigory kindled the stove and baked some flat unleavened cakes. I provided what was left of my tea and we had a pleasant supper. Looking into Grigory's lined face in the shimmering light of the stove, I realized who he was, or who I had subliminally taken him for when I first encountered him. Grigory Veselov was the old man I had seen that fateful night back in St. Petersburg in my vision under the table at the party—the vision because of which I decided to go to the Kamchatcka Peninsula and met Tausha instead. Things had come full circle. Here he was, the very man whose image I had taken as a model for what I wanted to become myself.

Veselov had spent thirty-seven years in these mountains and, as he confided to me, would hardly be able to live among people again. He also said that little things that were of no significance before had become of great value to him, and he had no desire to return. Things happened at such a different scale alone in the mountains. A view of a butterfly dancing or a leak in a kettle might fill a day.

I asked Grigory whether he had ever been lonesome. He smothered a smile and said, "No. I have enough companionship here. Sometimes I talk for days on end." I assumed an understanding expression, without really understanding what he meant. Without my asking him to, he told me his life story. It struck me as very odd.

Grigory was eighteen and engaged to be married when the Great Patriotic War against the Nazis broke out. He was called to the Red Army and had to leave his fiancée Anna behind. Before long, a terrible error occurred, and the Veselovs were sent a "killed in combat" notice. Anna refused to believe that Grigory was dead and despite everything went on waiting for him to return. The neighbors thought she was crazy. For three long years Anna kept gazing down the village road, day in and day out. But the day Grigory actually did arrive home safe and sound and knocked on her window—she refused to open the door.

The recluse paused.

"Why on earth did she do that?" I could not refrain from asking.

"An enigmatic Russian soul," Veselov said with a sigh. I could see that the pain hadn't loosened its grip on him despite all these years.

The meaning of Anna's deed never emerged, and when it became clear that she was not going to speak to him, Grigory, heartbroken, left his village for good. A dream guided him to the Caucasus. He found his cave and became a hermit. He did not tell me much of his years in seclusion, as though his life had ceased that ill-starred day when he had come home from war.

Having finished his story, Grigory made me a bed of hay. I lay down, and my last thought before falling asleep was of how the stove would keep burning throughout the night without our adding any firewood to it.

When I opened my eyes in the morning, the recluse was busy making some herbal tea. It was excellent. Sipping the steaming brew, I asked Veselov, "I gather from what you told me yesterday that you are not a religious hermit, but rather just a man driven into solitude by a broken heart?"

"Does it make any difference?" Grigory raised his eyebrows.

"Sure it does!" I exclaimed emphatically. "If you have lived here for thirty-seven years in search of the truth, you might have something to teach me."

Veselov gave me an examining look and said, "Come. I'm going to show you something." I got up from my hay bed and followed the hermit into the depths of the cave. We walked along a passage that was high enough to walk through without ducking. It led to another cave which was longer than the first and which opened onto the azure sky at the end of it and showed the silhouette of a man seated at the opening's bottom with his back to us. Grigory chuckled, "I'm not alone here."

The man was dead. In fact, it was a mummy. Completely dessicated, and with clothes practically reduced to dust, it sat bolt upright staring out into the sky with its empty eye sockets. I looked out over the brink of the opening and let out a cry. There was a bottomless abyss below.

Veselov patted me on the shoulder and said pacifyingly, "It's all right."

"Who *is* he?" I muttered.

"He's my predecessor. I think he is at least a thousand years old."

"Why is he preserved so well?"

"The air is very dry. And there is a certain energy here that prevents decay."

"How did you find this place?"

Gregory paused for a moment, then said, "I told you last night—I was shown it in a dream."

A strange thought came into my mind. I asked, "Was it shown by him?" I pointed to the mummy.

Veselov smiled, "Perhaps."

"And he led you here?"

"I would say so."

Emboldened by this confession that he had been led there by a dream, I ventured to speak of what I most wanted to ask him. "I also was led here by a dream," I said. "Many years ago, you came to me while I was in a kind of trance, and showed me these caves. Are you aware that you did this?"

Grigory smiled, but looked a little puzzled. "No, I am not."

"So you didn't come to my dream?"

He shook his head, "No."

I felt downright disappointed.

We returned to Grigory's cave, and then walked out into the open. The day was breezy. Grigory's grey hair and beard were flying in the wind. I felt it was time to leave, but my question about the motivation for his seclusion had remained unanswered. The recluse read my thoughts.

Slowly, he said, "I cannot teach you anything, but neither can anyone else. The knowledge you seek by its very nature cannot be imparted.

"You want to change and that's alright. Yet, look at the sky. Can the sky be different? Does it wish for any changes other than the changes that happen to it effortlessly day and night? Consider yourself the sky. Then what is left then of your longings? In reality people are like the sky, although they prefer to take themselves for ants.

"All the knowledge you have, you've acquired yourself and it belongs to you. All you want to know—you'll have to find out the hard way. This is how it has always been. Everything else is just words."

I was dumbfounded. "But books, teachings—is it all rubbish?" Veselov did not reply. He was looking into the distance where the mountains stood in their eternal grandeur. His lone figure seemed to answer my question more eloquently than any words. I had to go. We hugged one another and I picked up my backpack.

I started descending. To avoid backtracking, I decided to go down the mountain by another route than the one by which I'd come. Veselov noticed what I was going to do and cried, "Don't go that way!"

"Why not?"

"There's a *boy* there," he said significantly.

"What?"

"If you meet the boy, don't talk to him."

"Well, I wouldn't mind a little conversation."

"It's up to you, then. Goodbye."

As I was making my way down, I could see Veselov's figure for quite a while, towering lonely on the ledge. Then it disappeared for good.

35

The base of everything is the clear light shining in the void. Beyond that, words cannot reach.

I took no notice of Grigory's remark and heedlessly went downhill *my* way, but I soon understood that I had gone astray. I found myself in an unfamiliar ravine with a trail, which I pursued in the hope that it would take me somewhere I knew.

Heading on, I thought about Veselov's weird fate and his solitary path. I felt that there was some truth in his words about the impossibility of transmitting ultimate wisdom, but it was still my firm belief that higher states of consciousness are necessary for the survival of the human species. Tausha had provided me with a sense of direction, but a direction that we would all have to learn to move in or else perish. I had been given a map through hostile terrain and shown where and how to follow it; though indeed, the going itself was up to me.

All of a sudden I saw the boy. He was walking towards me along the trail. He appeared to be twelve or thirteen years old, wore a yellow T-shirt, blue jeans and was barefoot. The boy *looked* very ordinary, and yet there was something eerie about him, walking alone in this rugged terrain.

When we drew near each other, I said "Hi." The boy did not respond. There was no reaction whatsoever, as though he did not see me. His light green eyes were staring straight ahead and a strange languidness pervaded his whole appearance.

After the boy passed by, I turned my head and watched him walk away. Then I proceeded on my path, feeling somehow jittery. About ten minutes later I saw the boy again. He was coming *towards* me. Impossible! The only trail in the ravine was the one we both were on. The walls of the gorge were steep and inaccessible. There was no way he could have turned back to get ahead of me without my knowing it.

I stood there like a stuffed dummy, feeling downright terrified. Then I forced myself to move on, trying not to look into the boy's eyes. He silently went past me in the same indifferent way, like a walking mannequin. This indifference was his most appalling feature. But there was worse to come.

After a while I met the boy for a third time. My hair stood on end and I broke into a mad gallop, trying to give him the widest possible berth. All of my previous encounters with strange phenomena had been more or less in the form of energy, but this boy was a solid, material being!

I am not aware of exactly what I was thinking when I bolted. I just know that I ran for my life. Luckily, I spotted a shepherd way up in the distance and darted toward him, arriving entirely out of breath. Although the herdsman hardly spoke any Russian, no explanation was needed. The Georgian word "bicho" for a boy was enough. The shepherd offered me some fiery "chacha," which this time was very welcome!

From the herdsman's dramatic gesticulations I gathered that the boy had long ago been killed by a rockfall and from that time on could be found haunting the trail by anyone who walked it. He was the same in all seasons, and encountering the boy in winter, barefoot and in his T-shirt was particularly impressive.

The shepherd gave me directions, and I got back to Mutso safely, but it took me a couple of days to settle back into a normal state. I kept seeing the boy as soon as I closed my eyes. He left me alone only after I offered a prayer for his soul.

As the summer drew to a close, I grew more and more certain that my "leap into enlightenment" by trying to become a hermit was based on a self-induced mirage. The harder I tried to find my way spiritually in mountain solitude, the further my goal seemed to slip away from me. I left no stone unturned in my sincere efforts to break through to the Light, but, alas!—to no avail. The unvarnished truth was that I was as far from Realization as ever. At times I would hear a mysterious voice guiding me. I could not figure out whether it was my inner voice or an external source of guidance but, in the end, it did not matter. One night, when I had almost abandoned myself to despair, the voice said: *The sought-after truth is found by not seeking it.*

This message turned the tide. I realized that my longtime attachment to a pastoral yogic life had probably been nothing but a residue from some past life. Dwelling in a specific place as a hermit no longer seemed in and of itself to mean much now, and neither did my ego-rooted ambition to obtain personal salvation. There had to be another way. The place did not matter. But in one respect Veselov was right. The task was to realize onself as the sky.

The next morning I packed my stuff and left, much relieved at having come to a decision.

Back in St. Petersburg, the aftermath of my life as a hermit took a curious turn. At that time my girlfriend Irina worked at a biological station north of the city, and I decided to pay her a visit. We spent a wonderful day boating on the lake. As the night came, we retired to Irina's room. There were two bunks there. I took one, she lay down on another one across from me. The moment my head touched the pillow I was carried away by a powerful force. I was filled with an influx of an immense energy. My body seemed to have turned into light, and I lost all awareness of it. There was no pain, no weariness—not even a sense of weight. All this happened by itself, without meditation or effort of any kind. I was being propelled through a series of strange, unimaginable worlds that had nothing in common with ordinary reality. At the same time, I had a strong feeling that I was being carried in the right direction and towards the right place, and I wanted to fix the route to it in memory.

The only way to do this was to identify the unearthly worlds through which I was passing with something familiar to me, but the task proved impossible because there was absolutely *nothing* in these realms to correlate with anything I knew. My mind, in a desperate attempt to find any analogies whatsoever, began skidding like a car on ice. Everything was so *completely* different that all that can be said about these worlds is simply that they exist.

My innermost feeling now as I look back on this experience is that my desire to mark the path was wrong. It was based on greed and grasping and it would have been better if I had just let it go. Yet the temptation to memorize the path was too strong to overcome.

In any case, I was brought to an unfathomable ocean of primordial energy or, rather, to the shore of it. I stayed there for a very short time, yet it was long enough for me to see that this ocean is what everything is made of. It is the fundamental stuff of the universe, the base of all. I watched this ocean in a complete transport of reverent ecstasy.

My own personal energy was evidently not strong enough to allow me to stay there for very long, and I soon began to be rejected—with the inevitability (as I later expressed it) of a cork being forced out of a champagne bottle. The same force that had pulled me in was now dragging me out. My time had not yet come.

When I returned to the here-and-now, my body was still weightless and full of living fire. I opened my eyes and saw the room shimmering with myriads of tiny sparks. I had brought back just a minute amount of the ocean's energy, but it was enough to illuminate the entire room!

My dire endeavors to memorize the path to the ocean can be crystalized in this proposition: *as soon as all mental activity has come to rest, even the subtlest form of it, you immediately find yourself there at that ocean.* But the question is: how do you stop this mental activity? A thought cannot be terminated by a thought, and the ego cannot be melted by itself. There has to come something utterly overwhelming to wipe out one's petty graspings and fears.

I looked at Irina. She seemed to be in a trance. I had known since my times with Tausha that powerful energy manifestations electrify the space around us and alter the state of consciousness of those who happen to be near. I scarcely sensed my body, and just because of that, a strange idea crossed my mind. I wondered what making love might be like in such a state. To tell the truth, I had no sexual desire whatsoever at the moment; my motive was, rather, more like a naturalist's curiosity! And what followed hardly felt like a sexual experience at all. The keystone for sexual phenomena—bodily sensations—was absent. Irina's body was not matter to be touched, it was a gate to be opened. And so was mine for her. Behind these gates was heaving the same luminous, primordial ocean with which I had just failed to merge. We walked through the gates and met anew in the limitless effulgent space wherein the only possible way of being is to fly!

36

The time will come when everything serves as a gate to your salvation.

For years I had been puzzled by the absurdity of the lovemaking process and would ask myself: what is it all for? Though I had only slightly unveiled the mystery now, a startling discovery presented itself: that lovemaking was originally designed for liberation. It was only secondarily for procreation, and lastly for enjoyment. Obviously, the sequence has been reversed.

From that night on, I was unable to accept sex as the throne of mere pleasure. Ordinary lovemaking seemed to me more like a pig's bustle. But after a few vain attempts to repeat the experience I had that night with Irina, I gave up trying for a long time.

Shortly after my return from Georgia I resumed my healing practice. This resumption was inspired by my first encounter with Krishna. In 1982 the *Hare Krishna* movement was taking its first steps behind the iron curtain. The Krishna devotees asked me to let them hold a secret Kirtan, or religious service, at my place. I agreed, and twice my room was filled with the melodious strains of Sanskrit mantras, the flashing of orange robes, and the spicy aroma of Indian food prepared as a sacrifice to Lord Krishna.

After the Kirtan, I acquired a beautiful image of Krishna to keep in my room. I loved that picture. With a gentle beatific smile Krishna silently played his divine flute. The photograph hung on the wall above my table, which I used for various purposes including cooking.

Once I was chopping an onion on this table. The sharp knife slid off and laid my index finger open down to the bone. When one is injured, there is a split second before the nerve impulse reaches the brain and the pain comes. In that split second I instinctively thrust my injured finger up to the picture. I had never considered myself a devotee of Krishna, but my reflex action came about as a gesture of entire surrender and inner confidence.

Seeing the open cut, I was ready for the pain and blood to come but they never did. Instead, the wound closed up and within a few seconds it healed completely! Flabbergasted, I stared at the clean skin.

There was no scar. It was as though nothing had happened. It was a real miracle. Krishna had granted grace for my having hosted His worshipers.

This event served as a powerful incentive to recommencing my work as a healer, something I had been reluctant to do since I had been deprived of the flow. I soon became very busy. My word-of-mouth reputation spread. I had many patients—quite frequently too many. There were times when I would really get tired to death. But in the course of my healing practice, I discovered that there exists a special "reservoir" or "accumulator" of healing energy to which professional energy healers are connected. This reservoir has no limits, and the healer is solely restricted by his or her ability as a chaneller.

I do not know if that container has been made by gods or saints or if it is a manifestation of nature's inherent justice, but every time I needed energy for healing, no matter how played out I was, I got it.

I did not have any technical medical knowledge, and I could not bring myself to read books on conventional medicine. Whenever I opened a medical book, it would make me feel so bad that I would slam it shut right away. The anatomy atlas reminded me of a butcher's guide. I considered a man or woman to be a luminous being and my supreme interest lay in pure energy, the elixir of life that no remedy could match and no knowledge of anatomy and physiology could access.

The term "energy" is becoming increasingly misused due to the "New Age" popularization of spiritual healing. When energy is actually present it changes your life. Its reality is more evident than matter itself. It cannot be fabricated or falsified. It is like money—either you have it, or you don't.

I have noticed that sometimes, after a course of energy treatments, a patient can become addicted to the healer's energy and require further sessions as a "booster." To avoid that dependence, I began to experiment with various alternative methods, such as acupressure, acupuncture, herbs, hypnosis and others as supplements to sheer energy work.

Particularly interesting results were achieved by putting a patient in a trance-like state in order to extract from the patient's subconscious the optimal method of treatment. Some people prescribe themselves rather complicated remedies, others name individuals or places to avoid; some go into a detailed diet, and so forth. This method proved to be truly efficient because a person, as it turns out, knows deep inside how to cure what ails him better than any physician.

In the course of time I developed a system of therapeutic massage to cleanse the channels and remove energy blockages. Combining this massage with the energy treatment I started getting stable results. People stopped becoming dependant on energy "boosting"; instead, they advanced at their own level of energy functioning.

One day I got a telephone call from a woman entreating me to help her husband who was dying of rectal cancer. He had been discharged from the hospital and given two weeks to live. I came to see the sick man just to make sure that the diagnosis had been correct. I could see at once that the man was at death's door and that bringing him back was beyond my capacity.

The patient, a workman in his late thirties, understood perfectly the hopelessness of his situation and asked me just to reduce his high fever so that he might be able to spend his last days with his family in a conscious state.

I was deeply moved by the drama and, though my chances were very slender, I set my heart on helping the man as much as I could. I gave him an energy session and promised to come back the next day. But I never did. I had forgotten Tausha's warning that there are patients who are destined to die and should not be interfered with.

The next day I came down with an acute inflammation of the middle ear and lost my hearing for a month. The cancer patient passed on, as had been expected, two weeks later. I recovered, yet I am still hard of hearing in my left ear. My only solace is that I somewhat relieved the workman's karma by sharing it through my own illness.

On another occasion I had a patient named Nikolai who had old heavy burn scars all over his face. He told me the story of these burns. As a young man, Nikolai had served in the Army during World War II and had had to spend some nights in a trench filled with icy water. Since that time he had been afflicted with severe rheumatism. Two decades after his night in the trench, his car happened to catch fire at a gas station. Nikolai managed to get out of the burning car alive and was severely scorched, but his twenty year old rheumatism was gone forever! Nikolai believed that he had been healed because he had gone into shock.

Something about this case interested me deeply. I began to think that a most powerful self-healing energy can be released through a shock experience. Risky as it sounds, a patient can be helped to tap into his or her concealed power reservoir through the state of shock. I eventually ran across a few folk healers who use related shock techniques in their practice. Some of them call it "shock therapy" (not to be confused with "electro-shock therapy" used in psychiatric institutions).

The most outrageous of these folk healers was a man named Fedorov. He was actually an aged, retired psychiatrist who lived in the small town of Zaraisk near Moscow. One of his tricks was to chase a patient around the house with a saber presented to his father by baron Kolchak at the time of the civil war in Russia. A skilled fencer, Fedorov produced a scary whizzing sound by twirling the saber overhead so swiftly that it became invisible. He must have had exceptional stamina, for he would chase the victim to the point of exhaustion, until the latter fell to the ground.

In terminal cases Fedorov might prescribe that a mother sleep with her son or something similarly beyond the pale. In spite of his "shocking" methods, an endless line of sick people waited daily for the "procedure" at Fedorov's gate. This character reminded me somewhat of Rasputin, who used to copulate in broad daylight while making the woman pray in a doggy-style position before an icon of Mother Mary.

Another extraordinary folk practitioner I encountered was a petite old lady named Maria, renowned for her therapeutic massage. Maria refused to reveal her technique in the beginning, but I persisted and finally she communicated it to me.

Maria asked me to take off my shirt, then she gripped my wrist and slowly moved her clenched fingers up my arm until they reached my shoulder. The lady was half my height, but her clutch reminded me of a giant bird's steel claws. What was left of my arm beneath her fingers felt like a jelly of muscles, ligaments and bones all mashed together. It was painful, to say the least. But the demonstration was being given on my insistence, so there was no turning back.

Having mauled my arms, Maria laid me down on a couch and stuffed a towel in my mouth "so as not to disturb her neighbors," as she put it. I was ready for the worst, and it came. The lady somehow poked her metal fingers under my abdominal muscles and began massaging them from inside in a way I never would have thought possible. The final stroke was massaging my back bone *through* my abdomen. To distract me a little from the agony, Maria explained that a healthy body should be soft as a baby's. She said that tiny fatty tumors, spread all over the muscle tissue and which she called "little cancers," could potentially grow malignant. Therefore they had to be crushed.

"Do you work with cancer?" I asked, writhing in pain.

"Yes," said Maria with a wide smile, "I roll the tumors out with a roller."

Thank goodness I did not have cancer. Following the procedure, however, I felt much relieved, though only after I had taken a Russian sauna—which she provided! But later, an enormous wave of inner heat arose inside me and I sensed that it was burning up impurities.

As I left her house, I noticed a big metal drum beside it placed on a support. I asked Maria what it was. She told me that the drum was an implement for healing with hot horse dung. A fire is built under the drum and a sick man is put inside with the dung up to his neck for six long hours. I asked Maria what this method was helpful for. She said that it raised the dead. I believe it!

37

Leave caution about the body to its Creator. Only be concerned with the Spirit.

Maria was a disciple of Porphyry Ivanov, one of the legendary Russian teachers and healers of this century, who had lived in the Ukraine. He left a large following which is alive and vibrant to this day. Porphyry had been a sickly child who defeated his feebleness by making special use of the cold. As a young man he would walk for hours in bitter frost outside his village wearing nothing but his shorts.

Ivanov was a proponent of healing through ethical conduct and the power of nature. Cold water was his basic remedy. The first thing Ivanov used to do to a patient was pour a bucket filled with cold well water over the person.

During the Nazi occupation Porphyry and some of his fellow villagers were put into a mobile gas chamber. When the Germans reopened the murder bus, Ivanov was the only survivor. The deadly round of lethal carbon monoxide was repeated on him, but Porphyry lived through the ordeal again. As a result, he was taken to the German military headquarters and presented with a certificate, validating him as a "Russian saint."

Ivanov did not need any certification, though. He *was* a saint and worked many miracles. During the course of his lifetime spent in the service of his long-suffering compatriots, Porphyry attended to nearly two million sick men. He always worked for free.

Ivanov was persistently persecuted by the repressive Soviet machine and was repeatedly thrown into mental homes where he was used as a guinea pig for testing new psychiatric medications. Porphyry disposed of the toxic substances by "depositing" them psychically in his leg. As a consequence, in his later years he became lame.

All year round Ivanov wore only his shorts. Clad in this manner, he once came to Moscow in the middle of winter. There in the '40s Porphyry somehow managed to get an appointment with one of the top Soviet officials, Mikhail Kalinin, and introduced a project for "bringing the nation into a healthy state" based on "cold" therapy. The project was never launched.

Porphyry Ivanov formulated his essential principles in a 12-point declaration called "The Infant." This is an unsophisticated but profound manifesto. One of its paragraphs calls for always wishing our elders good health. In Russian this means simply to say "hello." The Russian for "hello" is *zdrastvuite*, that is, "I wish you good health."

Years later in Nepal I encountered another "shock-healer," an astonishing woman shaman named Lhamo. She is a Tibetan refugee residing in Kathmandu where on a donation basis she works every day with all kinds of ailments. Lhamo's vocation is to treat the poor. Before she became a healer, Lhamo had been sick and demented for eighteen years until she met the Buddhist lama, Taglung Rinpoche, who blessed her. Upon this blessing Lhamo was not only delivered from her sickness but enabled to work as a conduit of the Himalayan Goddess, Dorje Yudronma.

Before her healing session, given each morning in a room full of waiting patients, Lhamo goes into trance before a tanghka of Dorje Yudronma. After putting on an impressive shamanic hat, prostrating herself several times and invoking the Goddess, she begins swaying to and fro—and one literally can see how Dorje Yudronma enters the healer's body. In everyday life Lhamo is just a simple and kind woman, but in trance her countenance and voice dramatically change—her movements become imperious and powerful.

Having totally given herself up to the Goddess, Lhamo invites the first patient to approach. The healing itself consists of biting the patient on the afflicted spots and sucking out the impurities. After each bite, Lhamo sucks in and then spits into a special basin a lump of dark matter that looks like coagulated blood. This substance smells like vomit. Although the bites do not penetrate the skin, they may be rather painful, and some of the patients cry out. Sometimes Lhamo uses a thin brass pipe which she presses onto the body so that a dark brown liquid oozes out and flows down the skin. The healer sucks it off through the pipe.

Lhamo extracts from the body not only gel clots and liquid; at times she spits out tiny stones. The dark stones are to be dumped out while the white ones are considered to be auspicious and may be kept on the person as a charm. My wife Victoria keeps a few white stones extracted from her temple in a locket.

Amazingly, there is nothing that seems particularly mystical in watching this fantastic procedure. The set-up and milieu feels normal, almost like a routine. The human psyche gets accustomed to the ways of the supernatural very easily!

Lhamo's work is apparently an arduous toil. In the early days of her practice she used to swallow the impurities, but later she started spiting them out for the sake of the patients to help give them more conviction.

When the two to three hours session is up, Lhamo repeats her prostrations and comes out of the trance yawning intensely. She remembers nothing of what she has done. I do not know why, but it was this yawning that convinced me beyond the shadow of a doubt of the genuineness of the event. Not to mention a few basins filled with human dross!

When I had just begun to practice, getting rid of my patients' negative energy did not seem to be much of a problem. The flow cleansed me automatically. But when I was left to my own energy resources it became increasingly difficult to regain the energy I had expended.

There are two ways a healer may be affected by their patients' illneses. The healer may contract the same disease he or she is working to cure. The patient's negative karma literally jumps from patient to healer, as if having found a new home. This happens because karma cannot be eliminated directly but has to be worked out. It is possible for such a healer to consciously take on the ailment to burn it down himself. Mothers know about that when they involuntary take on the fever of their sick child.

The second way is where the healer unwittingly accumulates the negative energy and lays it in store involuntarily until his or her health simply collapses. This was true in my case. After five years of work I broke down. There was no particular sickness I was afflicted with— just nothing seemed to be functioning in my body any more. I was under the weather, nobody could help me, and I did not understand what was wrong. We had lost track of Tausha. I felt I had to do something in order not to give up the ghost.

One day an old woman came by and told me her story. During World War II she had lost all her family and, giving herself up to despair, resolved to take her own life. One winter night she heated her stove to the maximum, undressed and, having warmed her body, plunged naked into the snow. She did this again and again all night long in the hope that she would get pneumonia and die. Instead, the woman in fact was conditioning herself aganst the cold. After that night, she never even caught a cold again. I decided to follow her example.

It was winter time. With the help of my friends I found a housesitting situation in a small resort town and moved in. The winter was cold—the temperature would often drop well below zero. On my first morning there I went out in the snow with nothing but my trunks on. I spent only a minute with my bare feet on the frozen ground, but it was enough to make my soles burn. The next morning I spent two minutes in the snow, and each following day I added a little more time so that a month later I was able to stay outdoors for an hour. I walked, crawled, rolled in the snow, and rubbed it all over my body. I literally lived in the snow. I tried dousing myself with icy water too, but the snow proved to be colder. After being conditioned to the snow, I didn't even feel the water. The amount of heat my body grew capable of generating was enormous. In the evenings I would walk in my trunks in the park, scaring away retired old ladies in their furs. During my initial night saunters in the snow-clad forest I could hardly keep myself from running along the moonlit path, balancing on the verge of panic. But I felt I should not run and forced myself to walk slowly and with a steady pace.

The result of my snow retreat was not long in coming. I started to feel better, and in two months I had completely restored my health. I came to realize that it was not just the snow that had healed me; the human body is capable of enduring much lower temperatures. Rather, the *shock* of being naked in the snow triggered my inner fire to blaze up and consume the disease. Nikolai's burning car and my snow showers confirmed the same truth—shock can be effective healing.

However, shock is not the only dramatic means by which to release innate self-healing power. It can come from *change* as well. I knew a man named Vasily who led a rather insipid life as a computer operator. Vasily and his wife were typical urbanites. With no warning, the man was diagnosed with inoperable stomach cancer. His time was running short and he had to make haste. Vasily forsook the city, moved to Siberia, and took up a life of living and hunting in the vastness of the taiga forest. We met again a year later. Vasily had thrown off his cancer. He came back to the city just to bring his wife and children to the taiga.

38

There is no privileged path to freedom. Pitfalls await you everywhere along the way.

In the fall of 1985 I heard through the grapevine that Seryozha had committed suicide. A great sadness settled on my heart that eventually gave way to anger. Seryozha was the most lighthearted of Tausha's disciples, a sunny child shining with an everlasting smile. I thought that it was due to my gloomy disposition that I always regarded this smile as boding ill.

Since the collapse of the group at the end of 1980, the tide started turning against Tausha. He had to go into hiding because the KGB was after him. Tausha spent much of his time in the forest and narrowed his circle down to John, Seryozha and a few others. Not much information emerged, and I pieced together the whole picture only years later.

The undercover life they led was tough. They were down and out as they could not support themselves by healing owing to their concealment. At the time, the country was full of informants.

Worst of all was the loss of the flow. Tausha himself was shut off from the flow a year after he had cut me off from it. The laws of high energy are stern. Once given, it can only be applied in strict conformity with its purpose which, in our case, was its expansion. Having withdrawn from his mission, Tausha committed himself to meditation, writing, and painting. There is nothing wrong with this, but the flow was not meant for personal use. It was bestowed for working with people on the condition of total self-surrender. Tausha was not an enlightened being; he retained his ego, refined but not destroyed. Only one who has fully realized the illusory nature of the "I" is capable of ultimate sacrifice. None of us had been ready for that—therefore the flow ceased.

John abandoned the Chief a year after the withdrawal of the flow. Seryozha in fact stayed to the end. His unswerving loyalty was appreciated by the Chief but did not shield Seryozha from the dreadful finale. He was not a solitary player. Seryozha had the makings of a good disciple but was unable to carry on without the group and without being under the auspices of the flow. With the dispersion of our circle he lost the very context of his own existence.

Seryozha called on me not long before his death. I had not seen him for ages. For the first time ever I saw him down in the mouth. He looked unwell and weary. We played a game of chess which ended in a draw. I asked Seryozha if he would like to return to ordinary life. After all, he had a Master's degree in chemistry. Seryozha replied sadly that it would have been impossible for him after the taste of freedom we had been given. He was still pinning his hopes on Tausha though he did not speak of it.

Badgered, sick, and desperate, Seryozha hanged himself in the apartment that had just been rented for him and Tausha by a female patient and disciple. When Tausha got home and discovered the still warm corpse, he tried to animate Seryozha but it was too late. Seryozha had broken his cervical vertebra. Tausha called the militia and left. The militia came, drew up a report, sealed the apartment and left the corpse unattended for a week. Seryozha was ultimately buried in a potter's field.

I was not aware at the time of what had happened. I just had a vague feeling that Seryozha was away somewhere. Too far away, indeed.

When I learned the truth at first I was sad, but then, as I mentioned before, I flew into a rage. The forebodings of evil that I had experienced back in Armenia were coming true. I put all the blame for Seryozha's death on Tausha. How dared he play with people's lives! Was Seryozha the sacrificial lamb the Prince had exacted? Was the game worth a candle? Such questions kept plaguing me, but they remained mere questions. They did not foster inquiry or bring insight. In any event, Seryozha's death put another nail in the coffin of my relationship with the Chief.

After the news had reached Sevastopol where Seryozha originally was from, his father, a captain in the navy, left for St. Petersburg. Upon his arrival he went directly to the "Big House." That was how St. Petersburgers used to call the monumental, ugly construction on Liteiny Prospect built in the "Stalin baroque" style. The building bore no signboard, yet there was no need for it. It was the KGB headquarters.

The captain requested that an inquest be held. It was born in upon him that his son had fallen a prey to a cult, and the captain reported

Tausha to the KGB. The mighty organization redoubled its efforts in pursuit of Tausha, but it proved to be a difficult task because at that time the Chief had become a lone wolf. He lived mostly in the woods.

Forever homeless, Tausha had enough stamina to endure harsh Russian winters in a summer tent. Still, he had to come back to the city off and on to restock his food supplies. It was on such a journey that he was tracked down and busted. The KGB had grown furious, as it took them half a year to catch a man they thought of as just "some hippie."

Tausha was charged with heading a cult, violating passport regulations (he had not renewed his passport), being unemployed (which was a crime at that time), and vagrancy. On the whole, he could have gotten up to seven years in a penitentiary camp.

At the preliminary investigation Tausha was subject to cross-examination. Amazingly, he was saved by telling the truth. The investigator could not believe that Tausha had lived in a tent in winter. They made Tausha bring the court to the forest to bear witness to the site. Thereafter the investigation cast doubt on Tausha's sanity.

Having taken into consideration his pictures and manuscripts, along with the results of the interrogation of witnesses and Tausha's own words, the investigation came to the conclusion that the he was quite crazy. Subsequently, he was subjected to psychiatric examination. After a month in the KGB jail Tausha was transferred to a special mental hospital to judge whether he might be eligible for classification as being a person of "diminished responsibility." The mercy of the gods must not have abandoned him, as one month later Tausha was released on bail—a phenomenon that was virtually unheard of.

At about this time I went to see him. I felt that now it was my turn to help him. We had not seen each other for a few years. Tausha looked down-hearted and tired to death. He was not the person I had known. His wit and cleverness remained, but he was not a man of power any longer. I finally saw my Master without a disciple's conditioned vision. Tausha was no longer "the Chief." We were just old hands, brothers-in-arms, who had once given up their lives for the truth and now were bound by Seryozha's death. Was all that had passed what the Sufis call "going to hell in order to realize heaven"? I really didn't know.

Though we were both willing to let bygones be bygones, a certain nebulous aloofness persisted between us. I guessed that Tausha could not ultimately forgive my treachery, and I wasn't able to absolve him of Seryozha's death. Still, I felt that the bond between us had been cemented by something larger than a human relationship.

Tausha had no plans for the immediate future and seemed to be content to let it ride. I offered to let him recuperate at my parents' *dacha*. Tausha agreed. After that we developed a kind of strange companionship that was yet a far cry from the *esprit de corps* of our sometime brotherhood.

At the dacha, Tausha was unable to make friends. He did not belong there. He was a distant star whose remoteness made any reintegration into the humming human hive practically impossible. Tausha was *too* different. He was one of the few people with whom the best way to be is just to remain in silence.

I saw that the most feasible thing for Tausha in life was to be a teacher. Yet he could not teach without the flow. It would have been simply more words thrown into the world, not a teaching. The latter implies power over souls. Without it, mere words don't come to anything. But the flow was gone, and our own energy was perhaps enough for living, but not for work.

Over a period of two years we made several trips together. One of them was to the White Sea in the north of the country, Tausha's favorite region of Russia. Tausha was a northern man with distinct Scandinavian past-life background, although he remarked once that his previous life had been as an African shaman.

In the summer of 1987, things seemed to begin looking up. Tausha made a lone trip to Altai and returned in August exuberant and vigorous. I guessed he was considering the possibility of creating a new group.

Tausha described a shaman named Urde whom he met living in the Altai mountains. When Urde had moved to Altai from Siberia, he had been defied by a local shaman and accepted the challenge. The duel took place on the tops of two neighboring hills, upon which the shamans mounted and, facing each other, started performing their wizardry. After an hour Urde's rival dropped dead. From then on Urde was in charge of the area.

In early September Tausha set off on another lone journey, this time to the White Sea. He was expected to be back a month or two later, but as time passed, Tausha didn't show up. None of his friends was alarmed at this, for we still considered Tausha to be a law unto himself. Still a Disa man, he was absolutely unpredictable in his ways.

In October I had a strange experience. A cloud of luminous energy emerged over and a little in front of my head and stayed with me for four days. I knew with all my guts that this cloud was Tausha. During these four days I sensed his presence hovering over the crown of my head. I said to myself, "He's either died or become enlightened."

By the middle of December still no news had arrived. Tausha had carried with him only a month's supply of food and almost no money. At last Nana called Tausha's mother in Syktyvkar. The mother said that she had just received an official telegram. The telegram read: "Fly in for identification of son's body."

39

When newly enlightened Buddha Sakyamuni set out to preach his doctrine, the first person he met was a man named Upaka who remarked on Sakyamuni's halcyon and radiant demeanor. Upaka asked Sakyamuni who his teacher had been and whose doctrine he professed. The Buddha replied:

All vanquishing am I, all knowing,
Self-taught, whom should I declare my teacher?
I have no master, my equal is unseen;
In this world, with its gods, I have no rival.
I, indeed, am sanctified, am the teacher unsur-
passed;
In this world grown blind, I beat the drum of death-
lessness.

Shrugging, Upaka said, "Perhaps, friend," and continued on his way.

When John and I found out about Tausha's death, our immediate reaction was riotous laughter. We gave each other a hug, feeling enormous relief for him. Tausha was no longer bound, restrained, confined. We did not know where he was, but we knew for sure that he had been set free.

Tausha's body was found by a forest ranger in the deep woods east of Arkhangelsk not far from the White Sea shore. He lay on his back in his sleeping bag under his awning, as Tausha did not even have a tent. He was partly covered with snow and his eyes were open. There was still green grass under the sleeping bag, which meant that Tausha had died sometime in September or early October—that is, roughly three months before he was found. He was thirty years old.

The body showed no signs of disintegration, and no odor of decay had emanated from it during the days the body was kept in the Arkhangelsk morgue. On the morning his mother and a few friends arrived, Tausha's eyes were clear and no sign of mold was visible. When they came back to the morgue in the evening of the same day, his eyes were covered with mold. It was as though Tausha had been waiting for them to bid farewell.

The autopsy did not reveal the cause of death. It looked as if Tausha had died in his sleep for reasons unknown. I assume that he left his body at will. His mother transported Tausha's body to his native town of Syktyvkar and buried him next to his father who had died not long before Tausha's body was discovered.

So ended the life of my teacher, the most outlandish and preeminent man I have ever known. Though I had been Tausha's immediate disciple for only half a year, I kept mulling over his mysterious personality for years to come, trying to grasp the riddle of the power he had been given and lost. Amazingly, my apprenticeship continued beyond my physical nearness with Tausha thanks to this intensive thinking. So beneficial is any contact with a person on a higher level of consciousness, that even fighting with him means continuing to learn!

Although Tausha had been deprived of the flow and obviously could not live on without it, I do not rule out the possibility that he was killed by the same power, the will of which he had failed to fulfill. The more one is given, the more one is asked to give. There is no mercy in battle, and certainly none in the battle between Light and Darkness. Tausha once remarked, "The clanging of swords does not cease in Heaven." I am positive that if he had not abandoned the group work, he would have been alive to this day.

Tausha's death came in fact as an avalanche to me. He was a man who had flung the window open and made me breathe the air of another reality. Now I was able to appreciate the Eastern attitude toward the Teacher who becomes even closer to the student than the student's parents. The Teacher leads you to a second birth, more profound than the first.

I do not know a single person whose life would not have been changed by contact with Tausha. Even in his last years, already diminished, Tausha dramatically altered the people he touched. Once Tausha said that our work was that of the ploughman—we will be followed by sowers and eventually reapers will come. The beam of light will be their sickle.

After Tausha's death I felt myself on my own as never before. I saw no other way out of the "corpse of the world," as Jesus put it, but through meditation. In the course of the years of effort I had developed certain meditation approaches. Here are some of them.

Forceful Stoppage of Thoughts. Why should thoughts be stopped at all? Because the stream of reality is incessant, while the thought current is intermittent. The unceasing cannot be fathomed by the interrupted.

This is a tiring path, though the most comprehensible. The trick here is not to strive to eliminate the thoughts by means of thought— that is simply impossible. Water cannot be destroyed by water. Thoughts are subordinate to the will. Thus, only the will, if engaged, is capable of dissipating them. The engagement of the will means the involvement of the totality of one's being in this exertive meditation. This actually is an unceasing chain of efforts which resembles those of a man who is trying to get out of a clay pit. There is a chance, but it's very slim.

The Application of Thought is the opposite of the method just described. This technique is based on the premise that the Creation is an actualized thought of God. The goal of this meditation is to realize this thought. In fact, it is the realization of the essence of everything and, in particular, yourself. Obviously, this approach requires enormous concentration.

These two methods belong to the *active* type of meditation, which means using the awareness of "I" as the grounds. The "I" is not regarded here as an obstacle. An infinite number of active meditation methods can be applied for practical purposes. There are concentrative techniques for healing, protection, getting information, foreseeing, destruction, chanting, visualization, and so forth.

Among the active approaches I found the method of merging one's will with the Will of the Creator as the most powerful. I call it *The Merging of Wills.*

The major risk of the active meditations lies in the possible inflation of the ego. A sense of personal validity obstructs further advancement like nothing else.

In contrast, the *passive* meditation techniques are based on surrender, i.e. dissolution of the "I" from the very beginning.

Giving up to Shakti implies letting the energy flow as it wishes. The meditator completely entrusts himself or herself to the Power, being confident that the Shakti knows far better what to do and how.

A variant of this technique is *Surrendering to the Teacher*—if you have or are able to imagine one. A possible quick growth of laziness and irresponsibility is the primary pitfall of the surrender approaches.

A much more sophisticated and effective tactic consists of combining the active and passive principles. There is a part of us that *always* knows what to do. This is the inner teacher. He is not going to do the work instead of us but is forever at hand with valuable advice. The technique called *Listening to the Teacher's Advice* aims at the discerning of the inner teacher's voice and following its instructions. It should not be forgotten, however, that the inner teacher lives in the heart. This method has proved to have no snares except for distraction.

If the latter grows into a real hindrance, there exists the meditation approach of accepting whatever comes up *including* distraction. This technique is called *Total Acceptance*. You just take everything as it comes to you without altering it. If it is a distraction, let it be so. Factually, your perception consumes equally whatever gets within its range. The secret of this technique is not to choose but, remaining in a non-action mode, to ingest all kinds of grass on the field of perception unemotionally, as a cow chews on its cud.

Behind each segment of perception there is concealed a tremendous amount of energy. This energy is shielded from us by the moving pictures which we take for reality. As a matter of fact, everything we see is just a projection. If we place our focus behind the pictures, thereby penetrating them, the images will give way to what is forming them—the bursting-forward clusters of clear light.

The vision of the world as it is is supported by our interest in it—in other words, by our ravenous perception. We can satisfy this hunger only if we are saturated with the world imagery, with its tastes and sounds. Yet, if we enable ourselves to take everything as it is, the outer impressions stop being an obstacle.

No meditation is necessary when the wishes are illuminated and a man becomes like a dry tree in the barren desert. It is the arid desert that bears exotic fruit.

40

You do not die if you are fully aware that you never were born.

At the end of May, 1988, eight months after Tausha's death, a few friends who had belonged to the group and I got together at my place to meditate. Suddenly the meditation was interrupted by the sound of a door opening. I opened my eyes and saw Tausha enter the room and sit on the armchair.

When facing the uncanny in the past, I often had warded off my fear by taking it as if it were a dream. Strangely, I was not frightened this time, though I could see from my friends' faces that they were rooted to the spot with terror.

Tausha looked as he always had. There was nothing ghostly about him, yet none of us could bring himself to touch him. Tausha regarded us as though assessing the depth of our fright. Then he begin to speak to us, but without uttering a sound. Tausha was communicating telepathically.

He said that his mission on earth had not been accomplished and that we, if we were so minded, were welcome to complete it. He said that he had been spared and taken into the Light. The level he was now at would allow him to guide, protect, and supply the group with energy far more efficiently than he had been able to while in a physical body.

Tausha added that we could not evaluate the scope of his operation now and that the opportunity he was offering was too precious to miss. I replied that we would not like to repeat the dismal end of the first enterprise.

Tausha said that he had been allowed to call a new group that would be able to communicate and work with him. It was the first and the last time we would see him with our physical eyes. In the future we would simply be aware of him as a presence. He said that if we agreed to work with him again as a unit, we would be helping him relieve his karmic burden in the afterlife.

John, who was present, said that we needed time to think it all over. Tausha responded that he could give us twenty-four hours. I questioned what would happen if we said "no."

"Nothing," answered Tausha. "You'll simply remain on the level that you are on now." Then he rose from the armchair and left, noiselessly closing the door behind him.

Our immediate reaction was nervous laughter. I could not restrain myself from looking out of the window. Nobody appeared on the sidewalk where a person leaving the building would normally be.

Tausha's advent left us with feelings of rapture, doubt, and hope. When the initial excitement about Tausha's victory over the Grim Reaper quited down, there arose an explicit awareness of the hazardous character of the adventure to which he was inviting us. The following twenty-four hours did not pass easily.

We clearly realized the uniqueness of the proposal. We were being presented with a rare opportunity to have a friend *over there*, who knew us all inside out and was ready and able to help. None of us had succeeded in regaining the flow over these years—the mighty current had proved to be unresponsive to personal calls. Now we were being given a chance as a *group* once again. On the other hand, as Tausha had failed while in his physical body and had carried off Seryozha to boot, what were the odds that he would not lead us astray another time? But the hope of reliving the times we spent together as an outfit was too appealing to resist.

After twenty-four hours sharp, all of us were back at my apartment. Tausha's *presence* arrived as he promised. It was even more powerful than the advent of his visible self. The energy attending Tausha was overwhelming—an ocean wave that gently but irreversibly swept us up and carried us along. We did not have to talk this time. Our answer was clear.

Eight years had passed since we encountered the flow for the first time. This energy that Tausha was channeling now belonged to the same source, but it was more stark and overpowering. We discovered that the greater the intensity of the flow, the more meaning it reveals. The novel feature of the renewed flow was a powerful opening of our creative aptitudes. Painting, composing, and dancing came to me as never before. Above all, the flow now acted as a Muse, an inexhaustible spring of inspiration.

For the first week or two, the current apparently was busy cleansing my brain, for little stone-like balls kept coming out of my nasal passages. My sleep diminished to two or three hours a night, as it had been during the presence of the flow before.

My place became the headquarters of the new group. During the first two months, Tausha frequented my apartment every other day. Although invisible, he behaved like an old buddy. Sometimes he would even ask me to put on his favorite music, like "Genesis" recordings. I must admit, it was pretty weird playing music for a ghost!

On the other hand, we appreciated before long the advantages of having a disembodied guru. First, Tausha was always close by. We were able to consult him at any time, day or night. If he was busy at the moment, he would tell us so.

Second, Tausha, so to speak, no longer carried a big stick! When he had a body he never coerced us into doing anything, but, still, there's a lot to be said for being allowed to feel that coercion is out of the question. The discipline, as ever, was grounded on our free will and individual willingness. Yet the responsibility now was much greater. For instance, in the old days it had always been possible simply not to listen to a specific teaching if it didn't interest us, but our present contact with Tausha was essentially a phenomenon of *subtle hearing*. If we didn't *listen*, it simply wasn't there.

Activation of subtle hearing required rigorous training—not because it was hard to hear Tausha—hearing him was easy. But differentiating his voice from skillful demonic imitations, as well as from other voices in space or our own sheer fantasies, was a demanding task. These difficulties, however, pertained only to personal contacts; when Tausha came out for the group, no technique was necessary. The explicitness of his presence and the clarity of his directions were beyond question.

One of the modes given by Tausha to facilitate our connection with him was a symbol.

This is obviously the protective symbol *IM* crowned with an antenna. While the lower part of the symbol safeguards the channeler, the antenna tunes him or her in.

At times, when Tausha could not break through to some of us or one of us due to our inattentiveness, he would send a message through another person who was more attentive. In this case one's head would become heavy, as though suddenly burdened with a massive helmet. The chaneller would speak up if the person for whom the message was meant was around. Otherwise the chaneller would write the message down and deliver it to the addressee later. The message was always to be written down if it concerned the whole group or was of particular importance.

The profoundest way of communicating with our master was simply to dwell silently in his presence. We had been used to perceiving Tausha as a bridge to infinity, and now this bridge was in its purest, most effulgent form. We felt that there was such Might behind the master that we could not even begin to fathom it.

We learned to distinguish Tausha's genuine presence from our own fantasies rather fast. Tausha said once that if we doubted whether it was he or not, then it wasn't. As easy as that. Most of the times, however, Tausha's presence was indubitable.

We surely missed him as a human being, yet the irrefutable fact that death just does not exist, overjoyed us. Where was death's sting, if we were able not just to speak, listen, or laugh together with our deceased teacher but to penetrate through him into eternity?

41

A man had been looking for a Master for a long time. At last he met one and begged the Master to accept him as a disciple. The Master asked what the man wanted to learn from him. The man said that he would like to study meditation. The Master exclaimed, "Do I look crazy enough to meditate?"

Tausha made three people responsible for receiving and distributing the flow—John, Andrew, and myself. I thought it very wise of Tausha not to concentrate the energy in one person's hands. It was a triangle principle: in case one left the game, the remaining two, following Tausha's advice, would fill the gap with another man.

On one occasion, the Chief taught the three of us how to distribute the energy as well as how to separate the sheep from the goats. The hierarchical principle of distributing the energy is grounded on devotion. The degree of devotion, like a valve, automatically regulates the influx of power. We confronted the same paradox over again—the less there is left of yourself, the more you are able to convey the flow. The same principle is perversely used in the military as well as in other earthly power structures, though they use fear and aggression in place of devotion.

On another occasion Tausha described in detail how to program people. He explained that by an intentional, silent suggestion people can be urged or even compelled to pursue goals they have not chosen to pursue. The best time for programming is either in the morning before the person wakes up or over a meal. I asked the Chief what we had been programmed for. Tausha answered that the only programming authorized and empowered in our game was programming for the search for freedom.

Later, Tausha instructed the group to gradually decrease the number of techniques we were applying and to begin transmitting the flow in its purity through whatever we did—through speech and silence, through work and leisure. He wanted us to dispel the mysterious halo around the work so that the work and life would become indistinguishable.

Tausha did not want us to perform anything that seemed esoteric; in fact, he simply wanted us to be complete. At one point, Tausha advised us to stop using all occult or even spiritually related terms. "Nothing special," he said. "Just live on."

We were indeed working out a new way of living, which aimed at bringing the realm of Light and our reality together without building new churches or performing eccentric rituals. To perceive yourself as the Spirit and live accordingly is extremely difficult, because our world is still basically materialistic. For a person working alone, the true spiritual life proves to be next to impossible as it turns out to be fighting the entire world. That is why the saints, those infrequent winners in this battle, are so rare and precious to us.

The only way out of this dismal situation, Tausha saw, was to create groups that were integrated into the body of society, as opposed to monastic communities barred from the world by thick monastery walls. These groups would have to be capable of conveying the transforming Light, and not impose any formal ideology or structure—they would be meant to bring forward the Light itself, not just to talk about it. People must get the *taste* of living in the Light. That is what our work was all about.

This approach proved to be a true one. Not words or dogmas but the fresh wind of Higher Reality drew more people into the group than any kind of persuasion or entrapment. As one neophyte put it, "Watching you, I just feel that you know something—and I want to know it, too. That's why I have come."

At about this time, in one of my meditations, I saw a planet where inhabitants pursued a curious mode of life—they sat forever in cross-legged posture without interacting or speaking with each other. Apparently they saw no point in external action and just kept sitting. I asked Tausha what this planet was all about. He said that it is the place where people who are used to practicing sitting meditation end up. Seeing my confusion, Tausha added, "There is nothing wrong with sitting. Some prefer walking, though. It's just a matter of preference, isn't it?" Truth to tell, sitting meditation always did seem somewhat artificial to me, inspite of my own propensity for it.

As Tausha was becoming a part of my inner world due to the frequency of my telepathic communication with him, I came to realize how the gods and goddesses of ancient times had come into being. In days of yore, there existed spiritually powerful people who continued to support and instruct their followers from behind the death veil—exactly as Tausha did. This prolonged intercourse incited the emergence of religions, perhaps, even to a greater extent than the "gods'" very earthly activities, or the sacred writings they left behind. Tausha had no intention, though, of establishing a posthumous cult. When we asked him once, half-jokingly, what he thought of becoming a modern Russian deity, Tausha just swore in reply.

Though Tausha never mentioned anything about how long he would be available to instruct us, I felt certain that he would not always be with us, but that once the work was accomplished, he would take wing to the Green country from which he had come.

Tausha did not let us reveal his identity to the new group members. He said that our pursuit was the widening of the flow and his identity as a conduit had no special meaning. If we failed, the flow would find other channelers through whom to pour itself out onto the earth. Tausha placed special emphasis on the fact that our historical period was a crucial one, and that the future of humankind was trembling in the balance.

Amazingly, my demonic encounters simply ceased to occur. Tausha remarked that we had grown up enough not to attract these nightmarish creatures, simply by our having lost our interest in them. On the other hand, our intense communion with Tausha opened us up to contacts with many beings, hierarchies, and worlds that had been sealed from us before. It was an astounding discovery. The universe turns out to be teeming with intelligent life practically "next door" to our ordinary world—intelligent life which is ready for communication with us, and, sometimes, to give us help.

Another interesting aspect of the second group's work was the enhanced power of words. I noticed that a casual phrase, spoken in the flow with determination, often turned into reality. It made us more cautious about what we were saying.

Moreover, many of my subconscious, sometimes half-forgotten wishes started coming true without any effort on my part. The returned flow was a wealth untold in itself, and more—life began to unfold like a wish-fulfilling jewel!

Somewhat concerned by this spontaneous fulfillment of my wishes, I asked Tausha what was going on. He said that I subconsciously used the flow for achieving my personal ambitions and satisfying my particular desires. When I denied this, Tausha laughed but insisted that I did use the flow for achieving my aspirations. He said that the energy stock was unlimited and there was nothing wrong about my involuntary magic—as long as I did not neglect the work.

Then Tausha said that as a matter of fact our unfulfilled wishes stand in the way of Realization. There is no point in suppressing them. To deal with our desires we either have to satisfy them or realize their futility. In any event, the wishes ultimately have to fall away so that we stop dissipating the precious energy of the flow, for the amount of energy required for liberation is enormous.

I asked what was the point of saving the energy since the flow stock was limitless. Tausha replied that the flow energy did not belong to us as such. Using the flow for fulfilling our wishes was not what the flow was meant for.

In some group members the flow uncovered individual ESP abilities, sometimes quite peculiar ones. One night Andrew, while spending the night in his home, could not fall asleep and went out onto the balcony for a smoke. When he returned to the room, he discovered that his bed was occupied. Upon looking closely at the sleeping person, Andrew realized that it was himself! Flabbergasted, Andrew understood that, as a matter of fact, he was in his subtle body watching his physical counterpart. It struck him as odd that he had not noticed the difference from the very beginning and that he had even been able to indulge in smoking. In any case, Andrew realized that he would somehow have to get back into his physical body, but this turned out to be rather difficult. Eventually, after a number of unsuccessful attempts, he managed to reenter his physical body through the legs. Since then Andrew has developed a mastery over leaving his body at will. Tausha, however, forbade him to teach others this skill. The Chief said that the risk of not being able to get back into the body was too great.

Nelli acquired a strange psychic gift that we called the "automatism of hands." It was disclosed when Nelli and I dropped by to see a friend. We were drinking tea in the kitchen when the friend's cat suddenly jumped out the window. We were on the fifth floor, so we thought the cat's chances of survival were slim.

We all rushed down into the yard. The cat was nowhere in sight. We assumed that it had hurt itself badly and crept away under some bush to die. But Nelli spontaneously spread her hands apart and, moving her palms with outstretched fingers as locators, started to walk—straight to a bush, two blocks away, under which the cat was sitting, shivering but quite safe and sound.

Later on, Nelli developed a phenomenal proficiency in programing her hands to do unthinkable tasks. For example, she could take down the text of a TV program while talking with you on a different subject at the same time. Or, by putting her fingers on a map, she could spot a person's location at any given moment, merely by having touched his or her photograph or belongings beforehand.

Those tricks, however, were nothing in comparison with the expansion of the flow and the joy we experienced because of it. The number of people we managed to draw in kept growing. New groups began to emerge in other cities. Our outfit stopped being a closed circle and splashed out into the boiling revival of Russian spirituality.

Times changed quickly and there was no longer a hazard in being involved in spiritual activity. Russian socialism had had its day, at least in the repressive form familiar to us. Seventy years of Bolshevism were over, and the country was rapidly adopting new ways of freedom. The iron curtain had been withdrawn, and the fresh winds from all over the world were sweeping across my country. I felt that the time of the group's mission was drawing to a close, but this time there was nothing bitter about it.

42

Enough said. Now act.

No formal organization evolved from our group, although a multitude of spiritual and religious associations, movements and alliances was mushrooming throughout the country. Over time it became quite clear that our work had begun bearing fruit. Many would-be voyagers were indeed finding their way through the doors we had opened.

Some of the people who had encountered the flow through us remained faithful to their former beliefs, since we forced no ideology on anyone. Many more shared our way of thinking about "bringing down the Light" by means of direct experience—whatever they chose to call it. There was no name given to this sacred intervention, and for many the anonymous Mediator would forever remain behind the scenes.

As soon as the work began achieving its end, Tausha, little by little, distanced himself from being involved in any form of social activity. His evolution drove him farther up onto the higher planes of existence, and we enjoyed Tausha's immediate proximity less and less frequently. Nevertheless, he continued to be in touch with a handful of his closest followers, always ready to help with energy or advice.

A few people, including my wife Victoria, who had never known Tausha in his earthly life, were introduced to the Master in his afterlife. The staggering example of their developing relationship has served as further, incontestable evidence of the conditional character of death.

Once we asked Tausha how long he would stay with us.

"I'll stay as long as you remember me," was his reply.

As years rolled on, there came something higher than the flow. It was *The Presence*. This word is commonly associated with a person or a fleeting feeling of a person's nearness. The Presence I experienced was utterly impersonal. It was neither Somebody nor Something's closeness, nor was it the intensification of my own attentiveness. It was *The Presence*—a sheer totality of forever existing impersonal Awareness. Despite its impersonality, this Awareness was the most caring, loving and supportive thing I have ever encountered. It is Home.

This Presence somehow has to do with space. In fact, it is a boundless luminous space, virgin and, at the same time, perpetually pregnant with an infinite potentiality for creation. Imbued with quiet and peace, this space, nonetheless, seems to be the heart of self-unfolding creativity. Whatever one can imagine as well as that which is beyond anything imaginable, lies there in embryo.

Clear of anything fragmentary, the Presence appeared to be absolute completeness, yet devoid of any trace of staleness or stagnation. An all-embracing breeze of pristine freshness sweeps through this radiant space. Drinking in its zephyr, one comes to realize that it is the very breath of eternity.

This Presence does not feel like something different from myself; moreover, it pertains to my innermost nature. It is not "me" in the usual sense; rather, it is the nucleus of my inner reality, my sacral core. Still, this core does not seem to be pariticularly "mine." It is the essence of the Universe as well as of myself.

A striking feature of the Presence is its "normality." It has nothing to do with trance or ecstasy. The greatest Mystery has proved to have nothing mysterious about it. It is as ordinary as the words on this page.

For many years, I had regarded meditation as a basic means of liberation. In fact, I substituted meditation for the Way. As it turned out, the Truth lay not in meditation but in understanding. No meditation, concentration, or prayer could get me there, simply because there is no "there." All of it is being right here and now, an unseen treasure underneath everyone's feet.

If we try to summarize all of the instructions ever given on the Path, the shortest and the most universal formula would be—"Be calm." Or, as Tausha used to put it, "Cool down."

Initially, the Presence always came by itself. No attempt helped it happen and the slightest effort seemed to make it vanish. In this regard, the Presence reminded me of an easily frightened bird, ever ready to fly away. A state of alert non-action appeared to be the attitude most relevant to it, but, still, the Presence always *occurred* as opposed to being *achieved*.

As absurd as it sounds, the Presence is not "something" to gain or even to think of. It is non-graspable in its essence.

In the course of time, however, the tangibility of the Presence grew on and, ultimately, its overwhelming reality has surpassed anything in the phenomenal world. The Presence has become the most genuine, dependable and intimate friend I know.

In the Presence nothing remains to yearn for, avoid, or try to be. All of my cravings and attempts "to break through" look so childish and beside the point to me now.

Before everything else I realize that, in reality, there is nothing to seek or aspire to. The seeker and the sought-after have already met at the beginning of time and have been inseparable ever after. We are *already* there. A drop returning back to the ocean evanesces forever, yet the water is all the same.

It should not be inferred, however, that my consciousness, after a series of profound mystical experiences, has, at last, merged with something lofty and beautiful. Nothing of the kind. It was my same every-day consciousness—shallow, jittery and forever unsatisfied that has turned out to be what the Hindus mean when they say "Tat Tvam Asi"—"You Are That."

Look closely. The shining immortal Presence is right here and now— as it has ever been and will always be. It is nothing else but Yourself. *So be it.*

Montreal, Mission
Canada
1995-1997